V.D. NABOKOV

THE PROVISIONAL GOVERNMENT

edited by Andrew Field

with an introduction by
Richard Pipes

THE PROVISIONAL GOVERNMENT

by
V.D. NABOKOV

A HALSTED PRESS BOOK

JOHN WILEY & SONS
New York—Toronto

Registered in Australia for transmission by post as a book

National Library of Australia card number and ISBN 0 7022 0718 7

Set in Times Roman 10 pt and printed on University Text Printing 106 gsm. Printed and bound by Watson Ferguson & Co. South Brisbane

Published in the U.S.A., Canada and Latin America by Halsted Press, a Division of John Wiley & Sons, Inc., New York

ISBN 0 470-62805-7
Library of Congress Catalog Card No. 72-9252

PREFACE

1970 Is THE CENTENARY YEAR of the birth of two Russians, Vladimir Ilich Ulyanov and Vladimir Dmitrievich Nabokov. The former, for better or worse, is remembered; it is well then to consider the character and historical role of V. D. Nabokov, a jurist and statesman who would certainly have been an important figure in the other, the democratic Russia which in 1917 succumbed so rapidly that it is assumed by some that it was never more than a chimerical hope. Perhaps. There were, of course, raging and inchoate forces abroad in the Russian empire in 1917. But that there was also a sophisticated democratic presence should not be doubted. The Dumas, which attempted to establish parliamentary democracy within the monarchical order, were not merely elective bodies, but large elective bodies with widespread popular support in the nation. V. D. Nabokov was an important member of a major pre-revolutionary democratic party, and would be an exemplary representative of the short-lived Russian democracy, but for the fact that one hesitates to speak of him in simple political categories. Though he did not disdain politics, his stature derives from a propensity to follow dictates other than political ones. In this V. D. Nabokov stands with those public figures—there are not so very many in any country's history—for whom principle is more important than mere power.

V. D. Nabokov raised his voice early and firmly against the monarchy, but partially because of this he found himself conscripted into the Tsar's service—the military—rather than free to be active in politics at the time of the revolution. And, partially owing to this circumstance, his role in the Provisional Government was to be that of chronicler. His record of this critical moment in history is also a fitting monument to the man himself. *The Provisional Government* was praised not only by the Provisional Government's Foreign Minister, Pavel Miliukov, who called it one of the essential documents necessary to understand the Russian revolution, but also by a figure as remote from Nabokov, in character as in politics, as Leon Trotsky.

The patrician aloofness and correctness of V. D. Nabokov's public manner, which, various memoirists inform us, sometimes hindered his political effectiveness, serve him well in his restrained but hardly "impersonal" history. His dry and yet somehow also passionate manner contains many virtues, some of them so strange that they may surprise us today. One must understand, for example, his moral commitment against antisemitism which was so fierce as to be contemptuous of even liberal avoidance of or diffidence about reference to a man's religion. Nabokov *fils* characterizes his father's position in the following manner: "My father felt so infinitely superior to any accusation of antisemitism (its official brand, or the even more disgusting household variety) that out of a kind of self-confidence and contempt for showcase philosemitism he used to make it a point—and go out of his way to make it—of being as plainspoken about Jew and Gentile as were his Jewish colleagues (such as Joseph Hessen and Grigory Landau) or the Christian but impeccably unprejudiced Milyukov." This isn't the common liberal approach, nor, for that matter, does one commonly encounter the rather touching if comic spectacle recorded by Nabokov of men demanding to be arrested on principle and at great peril to themselves. This was not empty gesture—V. D. Nabokov himself died tragically in accordance with these deeply held rules of honour.

The primary translation of *The Provisional Government* was done by A. G. E. Speirs in collaboration with N. Wasillief, and stylistic revision was done on the manuscript by my wife Michele and myself before it was given its final form by Mr. Speirs. Special thanks are owed to Mr. Speirs, in addition, for his compilation of the glossary of names at the rear of the book. The preparation of the manuscript for printing was done, in extraordinarily rapid order, by my Research Assistant, Miss Helene Crowley, and the University of Queensland's Russian departmental secretary, Mrs. Angelina Koksharoff. The transliteration system used is a slight variation of the Library of Congress system.

ANDREW FIELD

CONTENTS

INTRODUCTION

THE CONSTITUTIONAL DEMOCRATIC PARTY of which Vladimir
Nabokov *père* was one of the founders and leaders was the most
influential political party in pre-revolutionary Russia. It was the
Kadets who demanded and won for their country a constitution
and in the Dumas created by it performed the role of the loyal
opposition. Nor did their activity end there. After the abdication
of Nicholas II in 1917 they assumed responsibility for administer-
ing the empire. Subsequently, they furnished political leadership
to the White movement, and, after its collapse, did more than any
other party to keep alive the national spirit among the two million
Russian émigrés. If these facts are not generally known it is
largely because since 1917 control over Russian historical scholar-
ship has been exercised by a political party which detests liberalism more than any other political movement, and has done all in
its power to expunge its traces from the record. No, history has
failed those victims of revolutionary violence who had looked
confidently to it to vindicate them. The trouble is that history does
not judge: the judging is done by historians who are coercible and
corruptible, and always find the winners more interesting than the
losers.

Nabokov was intimately involved in the affairs of his party,
in its triumphs and in its defeats. Two incidents illustrate this
connection with particular vividness: they form at one and the
same time chapters in his biography and in the history of the
movement to which (in the literal sense of the word) he sacrificed
his life. The first of these incidents occurred in St. Petersburg in
1904; the second in Berlin in 1922.

MODERN RUSSIAN LIBERALISM was born in the 1860's, during the
Great Reforms, when the government at long last gave evidence
of a willingness to abandon bureaucratic paternalism and share
power with society. The movement enjoyed greatest support

among the gentry, especially the well-to-do, Westernized land-owners of the central provinces, but it also won adherents among the intelligentsia, including the enlightened bureaucracy. It was from the beginning a national movement. Russian liberals demanded a constitution and guarantees of civil rights not because they believed them due them by the law of nature, but because they thought them necessary if Russia was to be transformed from a weak empire into a powerful modern nation state. Unlike German liberals, they never served narrow class or partisan interests, but always viewed themselves as spokesmen of the nation as a whole. This attitude was a natural one in a country where the liberals alone possessed a political organization resembling a party of the Western type. It gave them strength, but it also proved a liability.

Although the number of their followers and sympathizers was larger by far than that of the more notorious revolutionaries, the liberals did not achieve particularly impressive results until the beginning of the twentieth century. Their greatest difficulty lay in the steadfast refusal of the Russian monarchy even to contemplate the possibility of a partnership with society. Historical experience indicates that in order to succeed, liberalism requires a modicum of cooperation from established authority. The respect for due process which is innate to all genuine liberalism paralyses liberals when they face the necessity of using force against legitimate authority. It is so unnatural for them to act illegally that in a protracted struggle against entrenched authority they invariably lose out to more radical groups, unconstrained by similar inhibitions. Russian liberals grumbled about the autocracy but they did not actively fight it. The spread of revolutionary terror in the late 1870's did much to dampen their ardor, for it raised a spectre more appalling than the arbitrariness of the bureaucracy, namely violence as an accepted device of politics. The liberals resolved the difficulty confronting them by dedicating themselves to practical activity aimed at the improvement of the culture and material standards of the peasantry. Such "small deeds" were perfectly legal and at the same time helped create conditions which sooner or later would compel the monarchy to recognize that Russians were a mature people capable of ruling themselves.

The majority of liberals probably would have been quite content with such work, carried out through institutions of local self-government created in 1864, the *zemstva*. But before long the bureaucracy closed to them even that outlet. Aware of the long term implications of what the *zemtsy* were doing, the Ministry of the Interior began from 1886 onwards to restrict both the powers of the *zemstva* and their autonomy. The result of this counter-reform was to persuade even conservative liberals of the futility of working for some kind of peaceful evolution within the autocratic system: even the most modest progress required a constitution and civil liberties.

At the turn of the century Russians who shared this conviction began to gravitate toward one another and coalesce into a party. Three groups were involved: *zemtsy,* professional people (among them, Nabokov), and publicists, many of them defectors from the ranks of Social Democracy. In 1902, with the backing of these groups, Peter Struve launched in Stuttgart *Osvobozhdenie* (Liberation), a fortnightly dedicated to the constitutional cause, copies of which were smuggled by the thousand into Russia, as Herzen's *Bell* had been forty years earlier. Nabokov also wrote for *Osvobozhdenie;* but since all the contributions, except those by the editor himself, were either unsigned or pseudonymous, it is not possible to identify those of which he was author.

In August 1903 the constitutionalists met in Switerland and founded the Union of Liberation, an illegal organization dedicated to the task of rallying all the social classes, political parties, and ethnic minorities of the Russian Empire under the constitutional banner. Its strategy called for a massive campaign of public banquets, demonstrations, and petitions, all acting in concert on behalf of constitutionalism, and applying such pressure of opinion on the imperial government that it would have no choice but to yield. The outbreak of the Russo-Japanese war at the beginning of 1904 delayed the campaign for half a year. It was finally launched in the autumn, after the assassination of von Plehve, the Minister of the Interior, who had taken it upon himself to stamp out the mounting dissent by introducing something very close to totalitarianism. His successor, Svyatopolk-Mirsky, adopted a more conciliatory policy intended to appease the moderate elements of the opposition. He spoke of a "New Course" and made all kinds of ambiguous statements which confused conservative liberals among the *zemtsy*, leading them to believe that the emperor desired them to speak up on the constitutional issue. In this mistaken belief they agreed to participate in a national *zemstvo* congress which the Union of Liberation had instigated and which was to meet early in November 1904. It is no exaggeration to say that the events which led ultimately to the Revolution of 1905 had their roots in a misunderstanding between the imperial government and its loyal supporters of a liberal persuasion.

Svyatopolk-Mirsky, whom the *zemtsy* informed of their plans, first gave them permission to hold the congress, then revoked it, and finally changed his mind again, authorizing it on condition that it gather as a "private consultation" (*chastnoe soveshchanie*). The great *zemstvo* congress of 1904—the Russian equivalent of the National Assembly of 1789—met in a mood of exaltation. It was widely believed that the government, by allowing the country's notables to meet and express themselves on the constitutional question, indicated it was seriously contemplating political reform. (The belief was not groundless for the emancipation of the serfs in 1861 began in a similar manner). *Zemstvo* deputies boarding trains for St. Petersburg were accompanied by crowds of jubilant well-wishers. Once in the capital city they had no difficulty finding the residences where the meetings were taking place (these shifted from day to day to give the appearance of "private consultations") for police agents, in and out of uniform, obligingly showed them the way. The Post Office accurately delivered congratulatory telegrams which poured in from the provinces, addressed simply "Zemstvo Congress; St. Petersburg". Thus a genuine revolution got under way under the eyes and with the cooperation of the imperial authorities.

The major issue before the participants was constitution and parliament. On both, victory went to the constitutionalists. The conservative liberals, who desired an essentially consultative legislative body, found themselves in a minority. On the last day of the congress the deputies assembled at the residence of Nabokov on Bol'shaya Morskaya 47. Here they formally affixed their signatures to a document calling for the establishment in Russia of a constitutional regime with a parliament granted genuine legislative rights. The solemnity of the occasion is reflected in the minutes and recollections of those present. When the ceremony was completed one of the deputies exclaimed that future generations would commemorate the great event to which they had been witness by a plaque at the entrance to Nabokov's house.

No plaque hangs there today. The once elegant building has deteriorated into a slum. It is difficult to believe looking at this drab cooperative that it all started here, that the ultimatum which brought the monarchy to its knees in October 1905 and ended the autocratic era was issued from within its walls.

SIXTEEN YEARS PASSED. The imperial regime had collapsed and power in Russia fell into the hands of a party committed to the destruction of constitutionalism and parliamentarism. The Kadets had failed to persuade the monarchy to honor the implications of the October Manifesto and by transferring legislative authority to the Duma and a ministry formed by it to create a broader base for authority. Most of them were now in emigration, in Germany and

France, seeking to find a political strategy suitable to the new conditions in Russia. The prospects of their return there seemed good, for the Bolsheviks were in great economic difficulties and confronting growing resistance from the peasantry. Émigré politics did not then appear the futile pastime that it often is.

Unfortunately the party was split. In the summer of 1918, while the war was still in progress, Miliukov, its titular head, decided suddenly and on his own to abandon the traditional pro-Allied policy of his party and side with the Germans. This *volte-face* cut him off from his colleagues, the majority of whom remained loyal to the Allied cause and cooperated with the Volunteer Army. The collapse of the White Movement in 1920 convinced Miliukov that he had been right. He urged his colleagues in emigration to disassociate themselves from the White movement and turn left, making common cause with the anti-Bolshevik democratic socialists. He wanted to wait until popular revulsion against the Bolsheviks in Russia toppled the regime and created conditions that would permit a liberal-radical coalition to take over. Any association with the discredited Whites would be fatal to such prospects.

Some liberals followed Miliukov's "New Tactic" but the majority found it unacceptable. At a meeting of the party's Central Committee, held in Paris in the spring of 1921, the opposition, led by Nabokov, defeated Miliukov's resolutions by a good margin. The party now divided: Miliukov s "left" joined with the Socialist Revolutionaries; Nabokov's "right" made common cause with the Octobrists and other moderately conservative elements to create a "National Union", an up-to-date version of the Union of Liberation. Nabokov's faction did not believe in the possibility of an evolution of the Soviet regime and thought it unlikely that the population of Russia would be able gradually and peacefully to transform a dictatorship into a social democracy. For this reason it assigned a prime responsibility to the emigration, which it viewed as the guardian of Russian statehood and culture. Since the "right faction" was in a solid majority, Nabokov, as its leader, became in effect the head of the Constitutional Democratic Party.

In March 1922, in a final effort to heal the schism, the party convened a congress in Berlin. Here Miliukov spoke for the left, Nabokov for the right. Unnoticed, assassins from an extreme reactionary Russian émigré organization slipped into the congress hall. They had come to do away with Miliukov whom they regarded as the main culprit in Lenin's power seizure. While Miliukov was speaking, one of them lunged forward, gun in hand. Nabokov, who was sitting near the speaker, threw himself on the gunman. Shots were heard; and bullets intended for Miliukov lodged in Nabokov's body, killing him instantaneously.

The Constitutional Democratic party never recovered from this tragedy and soon disintegrated. The assassins were apprehended and jailed, but later on the Nazis set them free.

WHEN I REFLECT why Nabokov and men of his kind seem so attractive to me, I conclude that it is because of the quiet, natural dignity with which they carried out public responsibilities. They had no personal interests in what they did, and sought to derive from it no personal publicity. They acted out of a sense of patriotic responsibility, pure and simple. Their lack of political "realism" (in other words, of political opportunism) elevated their politics to a higher level of human activity. They were admirable men, the Russian liberals, combining Western individualism with the intelligentsia's tradition of public service. Their liberal ethos was remarkably free of that element of calculation so prominent in the liberal tradition of the West. Russia owes them a great deal. Some day it will recognize this debt and perhaps acknowledge it with a plaque long overdue at Bol'shaya Morskaya 47.

RICHARD PIPES
HARVARD UNIVERSITY

THE PROVISIONAL GOVERNMENT

THE PROVISIONAL
GOVERNMENT

EXACTLY ONE YEAR AGO,* on these very days of the 20th
through 22nd of April, events occurred in St. Petersburg whose
significance for the outcome of the war and the fate of our country
could not at the time be fully appreciated and adequately assessed.
By now it is quite clear that during those troubled days, when for
the first time since the triumph of the revolution the hideously
ferocious face of anarchy was bared for a moment, and when once
again, due to party intrigue and demagogic passion, the Acheron
was stirred up so that criminal thoughtlessness, unwittingly aiding
the cause of treacherous political designs, presented the Provisional Government with an ultimatum and gained from it
disastrous concessions and withdrawals on two basic questions—
foreign policy and the organisation of government; it is quite clear
now that during those days the brilliant and victorious first phase
of revolution came to an end and there took shape the as yet
vague outlines of a course that was to lead Russia to collapse and
ignominy.

   This is not to say, of course, that during the first two months
(on the ruins of an autocracy that had nominally become obsolete
as far back as 17 October 1905, but which in fact had been
striving for fully eleven years to preserve its meaning), when the
foundation of a new free Russia was being laid, everything was
going well. On the contrary, in the first days of the "bloodless
revolution" a careful and objective observer could have detected
the symptoms of the coming disintegration. Now, *post factum*, as
one looks through the newspapers of the time, these symptoms

---

*This is written on 21 April 1918.

seem so unequivocal, so obvious! But at the time those who took upon themselves the unimaginably difficult task of governing Russia, particularly during the early days, obviously surrendered to illusions. They wanted to believe in their ultimate success; without such faith from where could they have summoned the moral courage? In those fatal days of April their faith was shaken for the first time when "revolutionary Petrograd" carried the vital question of Russia's foreign policy into the public forum and when for the first time the Red banners bore inscriptions calling for the overthrow of the Provisional Government or the removal of some of its members.

That marked the beginning of the martyrdom of the Provisional Government. It can be said that Guchkov's resignation and the sacrificing of Miliukov to the demands of the Executive Committee of the St. Petersburg Soviet of Workers' and Soldiers' Deputies dealt the Provisional Government the first blow from which it never recovered. Essentially, the next six months with their recurrent upheavals and crises, with the vain attempts to form a strong coalition government, the fantastic conferences in the Malakhitov Hall and in Moscow's Bolshoi theatre—these six months were one prolonged period of extinction. True, there was one short moment in early July when the government's authority seemed to recover after the suppression of the first Bolshevik uprising. But the Provisional Government was unable to exploit the opportunity offered and the favourable conditions slid past. They never returned. The ease with which Lenin and Trotsky succeeded in overthrowing Kerensky's last coalition Provisional Government revealed its inner impotence. The extent of this impotence surprised even well-informed people at the time . . .

From the earliest days of the revolution I was in quite close touch with the Provisional Government. During the first two months (up to the first crisis) I held the office of Head of the Secretariat of the Provisional Government and consequently found myself for various reasons and circumstances in quite close contact with it. Unfortunately I did not then keep a diary or any systematic record. Busy from early morning till late at night, I could hardly find the time to deal with the work that fell to me. Thus I have virtually no documentary evidence relating to this

4

period. I have hesitated for a long time, wondering whether it is now worthwhile to take up my pen, after so many months have passed, to try to write down what has remained in my memory. The difficulty of this task is made greater by the circumstances in which I now find myself, living in this remote "bear's nook" of the Crimea which has been completely cut off from the rest of Russia for a whole month and which has just been occupied by the Germans. There is nothing at hand to aid my memory except piles of *Rech'*[1] which I. I. Petrunkevich fortunately kept and has put at my disposal. These are admittedly a very valuable help, but they cannot, of course, reflect the sense of that inner political life behind the scenes which, as is always the case, directed and wholly determined the outward movement of events. During my two months as Head of the Secretariat of the Provisional Government I attended its closed sessions almost every day. And I was the only person there who was not officially a member of the government. I shall deal later in more detail with my position and the reasons which led me during this brief period of activity to become a mere observer and not a participant in the political "work" of the Provisional Government. All I will say at this point is that, as far as I know, no trace remains of all these conferences. I could not take notes during the debates because of their strictly confidential nature. To have done so would have caused Kerensky in particular to object, since he was always very suspicious and resentful of anything in which he could detect an encroachment on the "supreme prerogatives" of the Provisional Government. I had no time to write anything down *post factum*. I do not think any minister had the chance to make any notes after the meetings. It goes without saying that now, a year later, I have not the slightest possibility of rendering systematically what went on at those conferences.

Nevertheless, I have decided to record these notes. However meagre the material with which my memory has to work, I feel that it would be shameful if this material were totally lost. I consider it extremely important that all those who in one way or another took part in the work of the Provisional Government do as I am doing. A future historian will collect and evaluate this evidence. It may vary greatly in value, but none of it will be entirely worthless if the writer endeavors to satisfy two absolute requirements: not to admit consciously any falsehood (though no one is immune from errors) and to be completely and utterly sincere.

I have felt that this introduction was necessary to clarify the very nature of my memoirs and my own attitude to these notes. I shall now begin my narrative.

AS SOON AS WAR BROKE OUT I received—on 21 July 1914—notification that as an officer of the Reserve I was appointed to the 318th Novgorod Infantry Battalion (*Druzhina*) and was to report to the Battalion Depot in Staraya Russa. At this point I do not intend to give a detailed account of my experiences, first in Staraya Russa, then in Vyborg where the Battalion was stationed until May 1915, and afterwards in the little town of Gajnash on the Gulf of Riga, halfway between Pernov and Riga. At first I was Battalion Adjutant; then in Gajnash,[2] where three Battalions were formed into a Regiment (called the 434th Tikhvin Infantry Regiment), I became Regimental Adjutant and in the first year of war saw the preparation of the home front, a process that was probably similar throughout Russia. I think that my observations in this sphere are not entirely devoid of interest but for the time being I am postponing writing about this and everything that relates to my service in the Asiatic Section of the General Staff to which I was transferred from Gajnash in September 1915, quite unexpectedly as far as I was concerned and without any request on my part; I remained there until the revolution, which came when I was Acting Head of the Clerical Division of that establishment. If I mention my war service here, it is merely to say that from July 1914 to March 1917 I took no part at all in politics. Even when I returned to St. Petersburg I did not resume my journalistic work with the newspaper *Rech'** or my work with the Central Committee of the Party of People's Free-

---

*If one does not count a series of sketches that appeared as a result of my trip to England in February 1916 and subsequently were published as a separate book under the title *England at War*.

dom. I could not return openly to either because of my position as an officer serving with the General Staff. I had no desire to do so covertly, as it were, and besides, there would have been little point in any such secret activity. In any case, it is important for a clear understanding of much that follows that I state this. From the outbreak of war until the revolution I was cut off from the political and, in particular, from Party life and only followed its course from without, as an outside observer. I was quite unaware of the complicated relationships which had developed during those years within the Duma and within the core of our Central Committee. I did not know Kerensky at all, and my acquaintance with him was purely superficial—when we met we greeted one another and exchanged platitudes. I could judge his political personality only by his speeches in the Duma, and of these I never had a high opinion. Of course, because of my intimate connexion with the editorial board of *Rech'* and my personal relationship with Miliukov, Gessen, Shingarev, Rodichev, and others, I neither could, nor, indeed, wanted to drop all ties and in effect lose all contact with the Party and with politics; and I had not done so. However it was because of my isolation that, after the revolution and in the early phase of my renewed political activity, I was initially unable to understand the complex network of both personal and Party relationships which entangled, and partly fettered, the work of the Provisional Government. There was a lot I did not know and, therefore, a lot I did not understand. This had an affect on the role I played, as will be seen shortly.

I will now proceed to the extrinsic facts in chronological order.

On 23 February my wife was due to return from Raahe in Finland where she had gone with our son as early as mid-January and where she had stayed for a few days after our son's return, convalescing from bronchitis. I drove to the station to meet her and clearly remember telling her and Colonel Myatlev (whom we took in our car to his house in St. Isaac's Square) that in St. Petersburg there was considerable unrest, a workers' movement, strikes, great crowds in the streets, that the authorities were nervous and apparently confused, and that it looked as though no great reliance could be placed upon the troops and in particular the Cossacks.* On Friday the 24th and Saturday the 25th I went to work as usual. On Sunday the 26th the Nevsky looked like an armed camp; it was cordoned off. That evening I went to I. V. Hessen's, where friends and acquaintances usually gathered on Sundays. This time, I remember, I found only Guber (Arzub'ev) there, and he soon left. Hessen and I exchanged impressions. What was happening seemed to us pretty grim. The fact that the highest authority at such a critical moment were people like Prince Golitsyn, Protopopov, and General Khabalov could not but fill us with the gravest concern. Nevertheless, that evening we far from suspected that the next two or three days would bring colossal and decisive events of universal historical importance.

Returning home from the Malaya Koniushennaya, I was unable to go the usual way—straight to the Nevsky and the Morskaya—because I wouldn't have been allowed to go along the Nevsky. I took a side street to the Bol'shaya Koniushennaya, then I went via Volynkin Lane to the Mojka, over the Pevchesky Bridge, across Dvortsovaya Square which was dark, sprawling, completely deserted, and past the Nevsky along Admiralty Avenue. As I passed the City Hall I could not help noticing the large number of cars (10 or 12) parked in front. I got back about 1 A.M., filled with alarm and gloomy forebodings.

On the morning of Monday the 27th I left for work at 10 A.M. as usual. At that time the Asiatic Section of the General Staff was housed in the building of the former Chief Command of Cossack Troops, in the Karavannaya opposite the Simeonovsky Bridge. As I walked along the Karavannaya and came to the square I was stopped by a gentleman whose face was familiar (who he was I neither remembered then, nor have I been able to since), and he told me that there was shooting in the Kirochnaya and that a military unit was mutinying. I recall that he mentioned the Preobrazhensky Regiment. When I got to the Asiatic Section I received no further information. Routine work started, but it somehow proceeded listlessly that day. Nevertheless we (my colleagues and I) stayed the usual time, until 3 o'clock, and at 3

---

*Not long ago, in April 1918, Myatlev, who arrived in Yalta, recalled this ride and my story to me when we met.

8

I went home along the Nevsky, which was still open to traffic at the time and was crowded with masses of people.

By evening, as far as could be seen from the windows and particularly from the side windows of our tambour which over-looked the street and gave a view as far as the Astoria in one direction and Konnogvardejsky Lane in the other, the Morskaya had become completely deserted. Armoured cars began to roll past, rifle and machine-gun fire could be heard, soldiers and sailors ran by keeping close to the walls. Occasionally single shots turned into lively bursts of crossfire. Sometimes, though never for long, everything became quiet. The telephone continued to function, and during the day, I remember, a number of friends passed on to me information about what was happening. We went to bed at our usual time. On the morning of the 28th of February heavy firing started up again in the square and also in that stretch of the Morskaya between the Lutheran Church and Potseluev Bridge. It was unsafe to go out, partly because of the shooting and partly because officers were beginning to have their epaulets torn off them. There were already rumours of officers being assaulted by ordinary soldiers. At about 11 A.M. (perhaps even earlier) a large crowd of soldiers and sailors passed beneath the windows of our house on their way to the Nevsky. They were walking out of formation and in disorder, and no officers were with them. This crowd was apparently being fired on, either from the Astoria or from the Ministry of Agriculture, but this has never definitely been established and even the fact of the shooting has never been established, so it may have been invented later. Whatever the case, this crowd, either because of the shots (if there were any) or for some other reason, began to wreck the Astoria. "Refugees" from the hotel began to turn up at our place: my sister with her husband, Admiral Kolomejtsov, then a whole family including small children brought along by friends, English officers, then another family of distant Nabokov relatives. All these were some-how given room in our house.

During all of Tuesday the 28th and Wednesday, 1 March I didn't leave the house. There was a lot to do settling in the unexpected and unintentional guests, but most of the day was spent in numb and anxious expectation. There was little definite information. All that was known was that the State Duma was the focal point, and by the evening of the 1st of March it was being said that the whole St. Petersburg garrison, together with a few units which had come from surrounding areas, had joined the rebels.

By the morning of 2 March officers were able to appear freely in the streets, and I decided to go to the Asiatic Section to have the situation clarified. When I arrived I found in the first courtyard a big throng of officials, officers, and clerks. I quickly passed through to our own building but shortly afterwards received word that I was required to say a few words about what was happening. I went and joined the gathering. I was received with applause. We all went through to the great hall. I got up onto a table and made a short speech. I do not remember exactly what I said, but the gist of it was that despotism and arbitrary rule had been overthrown, that freedom had conquered, that it was now the duty of the whole nation to consolidate this freedom, and that to this end untiring effort and massive discipline were essential. In answer to various questions I said that I myself was not yet fully informed about what was taking place, but that I naturally intended to go to the State Duma during the day and naturally find out all the details and that we could meet again the next day. With that we ended the meeting, and the staff dispersed in animated conversation. I did not spend long at the Asiatic Section, where there was neither the chief, General Manakin, nor his immediate assistant, General Davletshin, and naturally there was no question of any work being done that day. When I got home, I had dinner, and at 2 o'clock I went out again, intending to go to the State Duma.

At the corner of the Nevsky and Morskaya I happened to run into the whole personnel of the General Staff on its way to the State Duma to declare its allegiance to the Provisional Government whose formation had just become known. I joined them, and we went along the Nevsky, Litejnaya, Sergievskaya, Potemkinskaya, and Shpalernaya. There were crowds of people in the streets. On all sides were anxious, excited faces, and red flags were already out. Just as we were passing the Anichkov Palace an old man, respectably dressed and apparently well-educated, spotted me (I was walking on the edge of the group) and stepping off the pavement ran up to me, grabbed me by the hand, shook it, and thanked me "for all that you have done", adding vehemently and decisively: "Only don't leave us any Romanovs, we don't need them." In the Potemkinskaya we met a fairly large crowd of policemen led by an escort, apparently from the Horse Guard Regiment's riding-school, where the constables had been locked up at the outbreak of the rebellion. During the forty or fifty minutes that we were marching to the State Duma I experienced an exultation such as I have never known since. I felt that something great and sacred had occurred, that the nation had thrown off its chains, that despotism had come crashing down . . . I did not then properly take into account the fact that basically what had happened was a military revolt spontaneously sparked off by conditions which were a consequence of three years of war, and that in this beginning lay the seeds of future anarchy and destruction . . . If such thoughts even occurred to me, I drove them from my mind.

As we approached, Shpalernaya was completely blocked by troops on their way to the Duma. Several times we had to stop and wait quite a long time. Cars were constantly crawling past, hardly able to get through the crowd. The square in front of the Duma building was so crowded that there was no room to turn around. There was tremendous pushing in the avenue leading to the entrance and considerable shouting; at the entrance gates some young people, evidently Jewish, were interrogating those who were going through; now and then shouts of "hurrah" could be heard. For a time I despaired of getting to the Duma entrance, and I lost my companions. At last, by squeezing and pushing, I got to the entrance steps. At that moment V. I. L'vov climbed onto a raised place set up in front of the doors, or possibly onto an open car (I couldn't see properly from where I was) and made a short speech of welcome to the military units in the square. He could not be heard very well and his speech made no impression at all. When he had finished and climbed down and began to move toward the doors of the Duma, the crowd poured in that direction, and the crush became even worse. I do not remember how I reached the entrance hall. I was at once staggered by the

11

unusual spectacle which the interior of the Tavrichesky Palace presented. Soldiers, soldiers, and more soldiers, with tired, vacant faces, rarely kindly or joyful; there were signs of an improvised army camp everywhere, rubbish, straw; the air was thick with a heavy mist, there was a smell of soldiers' boots, cloth, sweat; one could hear the hysterical voices of speakers at a meeting in the Ekaterinsky Hall. There was crowding and bustling confusion everywhere. Leaflets listing the members of the Provisional Government were already being passed around. I remember how astounded I was when I discovered that Kerensky had been appointed Minister of Justice. (At the time I did not realize the significance of this and had expected Maklakov to be appointed to the post). The appointment of M. I. Tereshchenko was also unexpected. I came across a journalist I knew and at my request he showed me the way to the rooms where Miliukov, Shingarev and other friends of mine were. We went along corridors, through small rooms, seeing a host of familiar faces everywhere. We ran into Prince G. E. L'vov on the way. I was struck by his gloomy, despondent mien and the tired look in his eyes. In the room farthest back I found Miliukov sitting over some documents with a pen in his hands. As it turned out, he was correcting the text of a speech he had just made, the speech in which he spoke for the preservation of the monarchy (assuming that Nicholas II would abdicate or be deposed). Anna Sergeevna, his wife, was sitting by him. Miliukov couldn't utter a word; he had apparently strained his voice talking at soldiers' meetings during the night. Shingarev and Nekrasov had similar unregistering, hoarse voices. The rooms were full of a variety of people. For some reason a very bewildered Prince S. K. Belosel'sky, a general, was there, waiting, so he said, for Guchkov. After a while Kerensky, accompanied by Count Aleksej Orlov-Davydov, the hero of the Poiré case, appeared from somewhere, overwrought, excited, hysterical. I think he had come directly from a meeting of the Executive Committee of the Soviet of Workers' and Soldiers' Deputies at which he had announced his acceptance of the Justice portfolio, and approval had been demonstrated by his re-election as one of the deputy chairmen of the committee. Just as Miliukov looked calm and completely self-possessed, so Kerensky, it was clear, was

12

suffering from a loss of emotional equilibrium. I remember one odd gesture of his. He was dressed as he always was (that is, before he took upon himself the role of "hostage of democracy" in the Provisional Government) in a jacket and a stiff wing-collar. He grabbed the wings of his collar and tore them off so that his appearance, instead of being smart, became as it were deliberately proletarian . . . While I was there he nearly fainted and Orlov-Davydov gave him something to sniff or something to drink, I don't remember which.

In the next room some military conference was going on. I caught sight of Generals Mikhnevich and Aver'yanov in the distance. I think it was already being said—with a note of disapproving scepticism—at that time that Guchkov and Shul'gin had left for Pskov. There was nothing for me to do at the Duma. It was impossible to sustain any sort of coherent conversation with people who were desperately tired. After I had been there for a while and absorbed the frantic and frenzied atmosphere, I made my way toward the exit. On my way through one of the small rooms I met P. B. Struve who, if I'm not mistaken, had been at the Duma practically since Tuesday. He was in an extremely sceptical mood. I had a word with him about the unusual intricacy and difficulty of the present situation. Then I left to go home.

On the morning of the next day, 3 March, I went to the Asiatic Section at my usual time. At the corner of Morskaya and Voznesensky I met M. A. Stakhovich, who told me, as though it were an accomplished fact, that Nicholas II had abdicated (in his own and his son's name) and had surrendered the throne to Mikhail Aleksandrovich. This was confirmed by M. P. Kaufman, the former Minister of Education, whom I met not far from Karavannaya. When I arrived at work I again found great excitement, with crowds on the stairs and in the great conference room, and I was asked again to explain the situation. I agreed to do so. All the staff had gathered in the hall and the highly respected General Agapov, the Chief of the Cossack Section of the General Staff, also came. In my speech I imparted what information I had (it was indeed extremely meagre) and said that the Tsar's abdication should also solve the problem for all who supported the principle of loyalty *quand-même*, and then, dealing with the task

13

that confronted us, I developed the thoughts I had expressed the day before concerning the necessity to make every effort in our work and the need for unquestioning discipline. Others, including General Agapov, spoke after me. The general feeling was positive and firm, with no noticeable dissent. I even remember that Agapov raised a few urgent practical problems which, as he pointed out, demanded immediate solution if regular work were not to come to a halt and the normal course of affairs be disorganised.

After spending a short time with my colleagues I decided to go and see the Chief of the Asiatic Section, General Manakin, who hadn't left his house owing to an indisposition. (I think he had phoned to ask me to come and see him.) It was marvelously sunny, frosty weather. I had hardly arrived at General Manakin's house and had a word with him when my wife phoned and told me that Prince L'vov had asked me to report at once to No. 12 Millionnaya where Grand Prince Mikhail Aleksandrovich was in Prince Putyatin's apartment. I straightaway took leave of General Manakin and hurried to the appointed address, on foot, of course, because neither carriages nor trams were running. The Nevsky presented an extraordinary spectacle: there wasn't a single carriage or car, there were no police, and there were crowds of people occupying the breadth of the street. In front of the Anichkov Palace they were burning eagles which had been taken down from the signs of court-appointed victuallers. I must have got to the Millionnaya between 2 and 3 o'clock. A sentry from the Preobrazhensky Regiment was standing on the steps of No. 12. An officer came out to meet me, I gave my name, he went away to get his orders and, returning at once, invited me upstairs. Taking off my coat in the hall I first went into the big drawing-room. (It was here, I discovered, that the conference had taken place that morning between Mikhail Aleksandrovich, members of the Provisional Government, and members of the Provisional Committee of the State Duma, ending with the Prince's decision not to accept the "succession" which had been foisted upon him.) Prince L'vov and Shul'gin were sitting in the next room, apparently the boudoir of the lady of the house. Prince L'vov explained why I had been asked to come along. He told me that in the Provisional Government itself opinions differed as to whether Mikhail Aleksandrovich should accept the throne or not. Miliukov and Guchkov were definitely and categorically in favour of it and were making this question the *punctum saliens* on which their participation in the cabinet was to depend. On the other hand, others were against it. The Grand Prince had heard them all and had asked for time to consider the matter alone. (I imagine that he consulted with his secretary Matveev in whom he had great confidence, and that Matveev was in favour of refusal.) After a while he returned to the room where the conference was taking place and declared that under the present conditions he was far from convinced that his acceptance of the throne would be for the good of the country, that it might not serve the cause of unity but rather of disunity, that he did not wish to be the unwilling cause of possible blood-shed, and that, therefore, he found it impossible to accept the throne and referred the final decision to the Constituent Assembly.

Thereupon Prince L'vov told me that, as a result of this decision, Miliukov and Guchkov would withdraw from the Provisional Government: "It's no great disaster if Guchkov goes; after all, it turns out (*sic*) the Army command can't stand him, and the troops simply hate him. But Miliukov must be persuaded to stay at all costs. It's the job of you and your friends to help us." When I enquired why I had been asked to come, Prince L'vov said that Mikhail Aleksandrovich's deed of abdication must be drawn up. The outlines of the deed had been drafted by Nekrasov, but the job was unfinished and not completely successful, and, inasmuch as everybody was terribly tired and no longer able to think straight because of being up all night, they requested that I undertake the task. Then he handed me Nekrasov's draft, which I still have among my papers, together with the final text.

At this point I would like to insert a parenthesis and momentarily interrupt the thread of my narrative to consider the question of Mikhail Aleksandrovich's abdication.

Since that time I have often thought of that moment. Now, at the end of April 1918 as I write these lines in the Crimea, conquered by the Germans ("temporarily occupied", as they put it), having experienced all the bitter disillusionment, all the horrors, all the humiliation, and all the shame of that nightmare year of revolution, seeing a tormented, defiled, dismembered

15

Russia which is far from made better, having suffered the beastliness of the Bolshevik orgy, and being convinced that the forces to whose lot it has fallen to create a new Russia are thoroughly unreliable, I ask myself whether there might have been a better chance of a favourable outcome if Mikhail Aleksandrovich had accepted the crown from the Tsar's hands.

It must be said that of all possible "monarchical" solutions this was the least preferable. Above all, it contained within itself an inescapable inner defect. Our basic laws did not envisage the possibility of the abdication of a ruling emperor and gave no guidelines concerning succession to the throne in such a case. But, of course, no laws can eliminate the fact of abdication, deprive it of its significance, or prevent it. It is precisely this fact to which certain legal consequences must be related. Since, where the basic laws are silent, abdication means exactly the same thing as death, then obviously the consequences must be the same, that is, the throne passes to the lawful heir. One can only abdicate in one's own name. An abdicating emperor has no right to deprive of the the throne one who has a right to it by law, whether the heir be of age or a minor. The Russian throne is not the emperor's private property or patrimony to do with as he likes. Nor can one argue the assumed agreement of the successor, since he was not yet thirteen years old. In any case, even if this agreement were stated categorically, it would be subject to dispute, and in the present instance the question did not even arise. Therefore, the handing over of the throne to Mikhail was an unlawful act. Mikhail had no legal title to it whatever. The only legal recourse would have been to adhere to the succession that would have been followed had Nicholas II died. His heir would have become emperor and Mikhail would have been Regent. If Nicholas II's decision had not come as a surprise to Guchkov and Shul'gin, they might have drawn his attention to the inadmissibility of proposing that Mikhail accept a crown to which he had no right while the lawful heir to the throne was still alive.

I mention this aspect of the question because it is more than a matter of legal hair-splitting. There is no doubt that it considerably weakened the position of those who advocated preserving the monarchy. There is no doubt, too, that it had an effect on

Mikhail's thinking. I do not know whether the question was discussed from this point of view at the morning conference, but undoubtedly Nicholas II himself had done most (although probably not consciously) to complicate and confuse the situation. Admittedly he was governed, according to the wording of the deed of abdication, by his feelings as a loving father who did not wish to take leave of his son. But however honourable these feelings may be, he cannot, of course, use them to justify his deed.

Mikhail's acceptance of the throne would therefore have been *ab initio vitiosum*, as the jurists say, fallacious from the very outset. But let us suppose that this, as it were, formal side of the question had not been taken into consideration. What, essentially, was the situation?

On *a priori* grounds one can advance very strong arguments that in the event of acceptance the consequences would have been favourable.

First of all, acceptance would have preserved the machinery and structure of government. The basis of Russia's state system would have been saved, and all the essentials would have been there to guarantee a constitutional monarchy. The circumstances under which Mikhail ascended the throne would have served this end, as would his personal uprightness and unquestionable nobility of character, a character without a trace, moreover, of a craving for power or of despotic habits. The fatal question of the summoning of the Constituent Assembly in time of war would have been obviated. What could have been established was a real constitutional government based firmly on the law which would have been the framework for the new constitution, not a Provisional Government nominally invested with dictatorial powers though in practice compelled to fight for and strengthen its powers. The great shock to the nation, caused by the collapse of the throne, would have been avoided. In short, the revolution would have been kept within bounds and the international position of Russia might have been saved. There was a chance of salvaging the army.

But all this is unfortunately only one side of the question. For his acceptance to have been decisive, there would have to have been a number of conditions which just were not there. By accepting the throne from Nicholas, Mikhail would at once have aligned against himself those forces which stood at the fore in the first days of the revolution and which sought to take control by means of close contact with the troops of the St. Petersburg garrison. By that time (3 March) the minds of these mutinying troops had already been poisoned. They offered no real support. The consolidation of Mikhail's position would undoubtedly have called for resolute measures—not excluding bloodshed, the arrest of the Executive Committee of the Soviet of Workers' and Soldiers' Deputies, and the proclamation of a state of siege in the event of resistance. Everything would probably have been reduced to proper proportions in a week. But for that week it would have been necessary to have at one's disposal actual forces in which complete and total reliance could be placed. No such forces existed. Moreover, Mikhail was by nature a man who was ill-fitted, or even totally unfitted, for the difficult, responsible, and dangerous role he would have had to play. He was neither popular with the masses, nor did he have the reputation of being an intellectually outstanding man. It is true that his name was unsullied, that he had not been involved in the shady occurrences in the scandalous Rasputin saga—for a time he had even seemed to be in opposition —but this, of course, was not enough to enable him to take the helm with a firm, sure hand. I can't imagine what groups would have supported him, either on their own or for higher interests. The Kadets, who three weeks later rejected the republican flag (I shall deal with this in more detail in its proper place), would not have been the support required. The Civil Service, the nobility, court circles? But these were not organized, were completely confused, and not a fighting force. Finally, we must take into account the general mood then prevalent in St. Petersburg, a mood of revolutionary intoxication, an unconscious Bolshevism which had turned the most staid minds. In such an atmosphere the monarchical tradition, which was, moreover, devoid of signs of spiritual depth, could not be an effective force for unity and solidarity.

I am formulating my conclusion, to which I came a long time ago, in the following way. If Mikhail's acceptance of the throne had been possible, it would have been beneficial or at least it would have given hope for a happy outcome. But unfortunately the sum total of conditions was such that an acceptance of the

18

throne was impossible. In common parlance, "it wouldn't have come to anything". And from the start Mikhail himself must have felt this. If "we all have an eye to become Napoleons", he had the least inclination of all. It is curious to note that he particularly emphasized his resentment at his brother's "foisting" the throne on him without even asking his consent. But, really, one wonders what he would have done if Nicholas *had* asked his consent beforehand?

I now pick up the thread of my story again.

It goes without saying that in the circumstances I did not have to consider whether the decision was right or wrong. One thing was clear as far as I was concerned: Miliukov must at all costs be kept in the Provisional Government, and then, with regard to the urgent matter for which I had been summoned, a clear, definitive, and accurate formulation of the Grand Prince's abdication had to be found. As regards the first matter, I promised Prince L'vov that I would make every effort and use all the influence I might have with Miliukov, intending to see him that evening in the Tavrichesky Palace. As far as the deed of abdication was concerned, I immediately requested the collaboration of that astute and careful specialist in public law, Baron B. E. Nol'de. With Prince L'vov's permission I phoned him; he happened to be nearby in the Ministry of Foreign Affairs and arrived a quarter of an hour later. We were assigned to a room belonging to Prince Putyatin's daughter. We were joined by V. V. Shul'gin. The text of the abdication was drawn up by the three of us, Nekrasov's draft undergoing considerable alterations. To conclude my account of the drafting of the text, I shall simply say that after we had completed our work the text was copied out by me and presented to the Grand Prince through Matveev. The alterations which he proposed, and which were accepted, consisted of the addition of a reference to God (which had been missing in the original) and, in the address to the population the words "I command" proposed by us were replaced by the words "I request". Because of these alterations I had to copy out the historical document once more. It was now about 6 P.M. M. V. Rodzyanko arrived. The Grand Prince also came in and signed the document in our presence. He appeared to be rather awkward and somewhat embarrassed. I

19

have no doubt that it was very painful for him, but he retained complete self-control, although I must confess I do not think he fully realized the importance and significance of what he was doing. Before we adjourned he and M. V. Rodzyanko embraced and kissed, and Rodzyanko called him a most noble man.

To find the correct form for the deed of abdication we initially had to settle a series of pre-juridical questions. The first concerned the form of the deed. Should it be considered that, at the time of formulation, Mikhail Aleksandrovich was already Emperor and his deed of abdication was the same sort as the document which had been signed by Nicholas II? But then, in the event of an affirmative answer, Mikhail's abdication might cause the same doubts with regard to the rights of other members of the Imperial family as those which actually arose out of Nicholas II's abdication. Furthermore, this would sanction Nicholas II's erroneous assumption that he had the right to make Mikhail the Emperor. We, therefore, came to the conclusion that the situation had to be interpreted thus: Mikhail had refused to assume the supreme authority. This, in fact, is what the legally valid contents of the document had to convey. But in the prevailing conditions it seemed essential not to be limited by the negative aspect of the deed but to use his statement in order solemnly to consolidate, for that section of the population for which it might have serious moral significance, the full powers of the Provisional Government and its continuity with the State Duma. This was done with the words "to the Provisional Government which has come into being on the initiative of the State Duma and which is invested with full powers". Shul'gin supplied the first part of the formula; I, the second. Again, from the legal point of view, it could be objected that Mikhail Aleksandrovich, in not accepting supreme authority, could not give any compulsory and binding instructions concerning the limits and substance of the Provisional Government's power. But, I repeat, in this instance we did not consider the centre of gravity to be the legal force of the formula but only its moral and political significance. It must be pointed out that the deed of rejection of the throne signed by Mikhail was the *only* deed which defined the scope of the Provisional Government's power and at the same time resolved the issue of its functional structure, in particular, and chiefly, the issue of the continuance of the legislative institutions. As is known, in its first declaration the Provisional Government spoke of itself as a "Cabinet", and the formation of this Cabinet was considered "a more stable structure of executive power." Obviously, when this declaration was composed, it was still uncertain what form the provisional regime would take. With the deed of rejection it was assumed that full legislative powers also belonged to the Provisional Government. What is more, on the previous day the question had been raised within the Provisional Government (in the words of B. E. Nol'de) of "the promulgation of laws and the taking of financial measures according to Article 87 of the legal code". It may seem odd that I have dealt with the contents of the deed of rejection in such detail. It may be said that this deed didn't make much impression on the populace, that it was soon forgotten and overshadowed by events. This may be so. All the same, there is no doubt that from a broad historical viewpoint the deed of 3 March had very great importance, that it was in fact an historical deed, and that its importance may yet become evident in the future. For us then in the first days of the revolution, when it was still unknown how the rest of Russia and allied foreign powers would react to the revolution, the formation of the Provisional Government, and the entirely new situation, every word seemed enormously important. And I think that we were right.

I have already said that our work dragged on until evening. When we came out it was dark. If my memory serves me correctly, I didn't go back home but drove directly to the State Duma to meet with Miliukov, to show him the draft of the deed which I had brought with me, and to arrange its publication in the press. But first and foremost, of course, I had to fulfill the promise I had made Prince G. E. L'vov to make every effort to persuade Miliukov not to withdraw from the Provisional Government.

I, of course, had not the slightest doubt that, if Miliukov stood by his decision, serious and possibly even disastrous complications would result, not to mention the impression of discord from the very beginning, the consequences for the party, which would be thrown immediately into confusion, and the difficult position of Kadet Ministers[3] who remained. With Miliukov's resignation the Provisional Government would be losing its greatest intellectual and the only man who could direct foreign policy and who was known to Europe. His resignation would in fact have been a veritable catastrophe.

When I got to the Tavrichesky Palace I found Miliukov straightaway. That same day Vinaver had already been talking to him about the resignation and had been trying to persuade him to alter his decision. I read him the text of Mikhail's rejection of the throne. He was satisfied with it, and I think it served as the final fillip which induced him to stay with the Provisional Government. Who influenced Guchkov in the same direction and when, I do not know.

As before, Anna Sergeevna was with Miliukov. From her I learned the tragic news of the massacre in Helsingfors and the grim situation at the battle front. She herself seemed completely crushed by these events. I was extremely shaken by them. At once strains of sadness and grief which boded no good began to obtrude on the joyful exultation. I must observe at this point that the conviction was promptly expressed that German subversion was responsible for the massacre.

To what extent the Germans had a hand in our revolution is a question which, I suppose, will never receive a full and exhaustive answer. In this connexion I recall one very nasty episode which occurred about two weeks later during a closed session of the Provisional Government. Miliukov was speaking and remarked, in what context I don't remember, that it was no secret that German money had been a contributory factor in the revolution. I make the reservation that I do not recall his exact words, but the idea was precisely that, and it was expressed quite categorically. The session was taking place late at night in the Mariinsky Palace. Miliukov was sitting at a table. Kerensky, as was his wont, was impatiently and irritably pacing the hall from end to end. At the moment when Miliukov uttered these words, Kerensky was in a far corner of the room. Suddenly he stopped and shouted: "What's that? What did you say? Say it again!" and strode rapidly to his seat at the table. Miliukov repeated the sentence calmly and, as it were, emphatically. Kerensky became like a man possessed. He grabbed his portfolio, slammed it on the table, and yelled: "Since

Mr. Miliukov has dared to slander the sacred cause of the great Russian revolution in my presence, I do not wish to remain here another minute." So saying, he turned around and shot out of the hall. Tereshchenko and another Minster ran after him but came back and reported that they had not managed to stop him and that he had gone home (to the Ministry of Justice where he was living at the time). I remember that Miliukov remained absolutely cool and when I said to him: "What a disgusting and ridiculous trick!", he replied, "Yes, that's Kerensky's usual way. In the Duma, too, he often used to play tricks like that, picking out some phrase used by a political opponent, then twisting it and using it as a weapon." As a matter of fact, none of the other Ministers made the slightest comment about the words which had sparked off Kerensky's indignation, but they all thought he should be calmed and mollified by explaining that Miliukov's words were not meant to be a general appraisal of the revolution. Somebody (I think it was Tereshchenko) suggested that Prince L'vov should go and see Kerensky. The others agreed. (Miliukov was taking no part in all this; he, of course, found the whole incident extremely distasteful.) Prince L'vov readily agreed to go and "have a talk" with Kerensky. Of course, it all fizzled out, but it left a painful impression. Incidentally, was there ever a closed session which did not leave a similar impression? But more about this later . . .

That same evening (3 March) in the Tavrichesky Palace, Miliukov told me that they were counting on me to fill an important new post and asked whether I would agree to accept the Governor-Generalship of Finland. I at once refused very decisively. Apart from any personal considerations, particularly, having to leave St. Petersburg, my refusal was due to my awareness that I was totally unfit to manage Finnish affairs. I had never taken any special interest in them, I had no contacts or even close friends in Finland, and I knew very little about political sentiments and Party trends there.

Refusing any administrative office, I offered my services as "Head of the Secretariat of the Provisional Government", a post corresponding to the former Head of the Secretariat of the Council of Ministers. I considered that this post, outwardly a minor one, would acquire particular importance in the new provisional regime, whose functions still remained so vague and undefined. In this area we were faced, in practice, with the tasks of setting hard and fast limits to government activity, giving the governmental process a proper and regular form, and also resolving whole series of problems which did not fall within the province of any individual Ministers. But apart from that—for I did not as yet realize the atmosphere in which I would find myself—because I was closely linked by Party relationships with a number of Ministers, I expected to be given a deliberative vote at the sessions of the Provisional Government. I shall later speak of the position which was created for me and which led me, during the first crisis caused by the resignation of Miliukov and Guchkov, to announce my firm desire to resign as Head of the Secretariat.

Miliukov could not but agree with the arguments I put forward. We discussed possible candidates for the post of Governor-General of Finland. At that time my old friend Stakhovich had not yet been mentioned, and I do not know who proposed him, but it was a choice which proved to be completely successful in many respects if not in all. I do not remember whether it was that same evening or the next morning that my appointment as Head of the Secretariat was confirmed. At any rate, on Saturday, 4 March I was attending the evening sessions of the Provisional Government which were held in the great hall of the Council of the Minister of Internal Affairs in the Ministry building in Aleksandrovsky Theatre Square.

During the first days of the Provisional Government's existence (Thursday, 2 and Friday, 3 March) there could, of course, be no question of an organized Secretariat. But some sort of office had to be improvised at once, and this job was given to Ya.N. Glinka who had run the State Duma's Secretariat. He used the staff of the Duma's Office. It should, however, be pointed out that the record of the first and extremely important session of the Provisional Government was quite unsatisfactory and even unintelligible. When I read through the record, I was rather puzzled and told Miliukov about it. When he had read it, he used stronger language about it than I. There and then it was agreed that he would take it and reproduce from memory the order of business and decisions of the first session, after which the Provisional Gov-

24

ernment would sign it once it had been checked in plenary session. Pavel Nikolaevich certainly took the record with him, but in his two months as Minister for Foreign Affairs he apparently did not find the necessary spare time to do the job. However often I reminded him of it he always gave an embarrassed smile and promised to work on it in the next few days, but even so he never fulfilled his promise. So the record was never used, and I don't think he will return it. This is why the printed minutes of the sessions of the Provisional Government begin with No. 2.

Here I will say a few words about how I organized the Provisional Government's Secretariat. First to be settled was the question of my assistant, the person on whom would fall the greatest share of the routine paper work. Obviously it could only be a man I could trust implicitly and unreservedly and who at the same time was to some extent familiar with the Secretariat of the Provisional Government. Clearly, the first of these requirements was not met by the then assistant (or deputy) to the Head of the Secretariat of the Council of Ministers (I. N. Lodyzhensky), A. S. Putilov, with whom I was personally unacquainted and who, moreover, was disliked by the staff. My choice fell on A. M. Onu. I had known him since 1894, had worked in the State Secretariat with him for five years (from 1894 to 1899, when I retired), and I had complete confidence in his loyalty and his willingness to devote himself to his work. In the second place, I judged him to have sound business experience as assistant to the State-Secretary of the State Council, so he would not be a *homo novus* in the Secretariat. I did not anticipate any prejudice with regard to myself in the Secretariat (where I met some of my former students in the School of Jurisprudence, Messrs. Karshbaum and Freygang), but at the same time I could not have expected, in the two months I worked with the Secretariat, to establish exceptionally cordial relations. I must place on record here that the vast majority of the staff proved fully equal to the work which required a quite exceptional capacity for work, conscientiousness, and "discretion". I retain the very best memories of our work together and of our parting, when I received from them an address couched in affectionate terms. As regards A. M. Onu, I was not disappointed either with his devotion and willingness to work or with the excellent qualities of his mind and heart. I should add that our personal relations always were and have remained excellent and that my feelings for him could only be those of sincere gratitude and deep respect. On the Saturday I informed him by phone of my plans for him and obtained his consent. My own position still had to be regularized. Obviously, my appointment as Head of the Secretariat of the Provisional Government was incompatible with my rank of ensign. As early as the evening of Saturday the 4th A. I. Guchkov for this reason signed an order which placed me on the retired list. On Monday the 6th I assumed control of the Secretariat in the Mariinsky Palace. A. S. Putilov, who visited me in the morning, introduced the staff to me. He made a speech of welcome, and I also replied with a short speech. Then I. N. Lodyzhensky arrived, and we had a fairly long chat in what had formerly been his study. But it was in connexion with Lodyzhensky and Putilov that I first encountered the problem of providing for retiring officials who had attained high rank, a problem which was later to cause the Provisional Government a great deal of trouble. Since I neither intend to maintain chronological order in these notes, nor could do so even if I wanted, I will deal with this problem now since it is raised.

As we know, during the first days and even weeks of the revolution, a favourite topic in the press and many public speeches —apart from the "bloodless" nature of a revolution which in its further course and development caused so many rivers of blood to flow—was its fabulous speed and the ease with which the new system was accepted by those who had appeared to be the most reliable and faithful bulwark of the old order. Among these were the Russian Civil Service, and, in particular, the St. Petersburg branch. I recall that as early as 1905, at the first congress of Zemstvo and urban officials after 17 October (held in Moscow, in Morozova's house in Vozdvizhenko), the possibility was raised of completely replacing the whole local administrative machinery (mainly governors, of course); the view was put forward that one could not expect from servants of absolutism either the willingness or the ability to serve the new system, and that they would be hostile to it and would adopt an attitude which in present-day revolutionary jargon is called "sabotage". At the time I spoke against this assumption. I pointed out that we scarcely had a sufficient number of ideologically trained workers available, capable of filling jobs in the complicated government machine straightaway; on the other hand, using a joking reminder of Kukol'nik's[4] famous words, "If His Majesty so orders, I can be an obstetrician", I tried to show that one should not expect from local administrators (from the majority, of course) a firmness of conviction, a depth of devotion and a doggedness that would resist an authoritative *mot d'ordre* from above—assuming, of course, the *mot d'ordre* to be sincere and "authentic". I. I. Petrunkevich opposed me at that time. Unfortunately, I was not there to hear the opposing speech in which he, making good and witty use of my own quotation, declared amid general laughter that he would not like to be a woman in childbirth attended by "an obstetrician by Royal Command," and that in such an event the mother's fate would be the fate of Russia. Notwithstanding the wittiness of this reply, I was not convinced by it. Now, the main argument put forward for not accepting the old administrators was their personal attitude and sentiments, not their lack of technical training (have we very many technically trained people anyway?)—and it was only in this connexion that my quotation made any sense. I meant, and I still think, that the vast majority of civil servants are far from infected with the urge to be *"plus royaliste que le roi"*, that they would be ready to accept a *fait accompli,* would submit to a new order and would not indulge in "sabotage". Of course, both in central and outlying organizations, in 1905 and in 1907, there were individuals unacceptable on principle and in practice to the new regime by virtue of their previous activities and clearly defined political outlooks. These had been removed from office.

The Provisional Government, as we know, acted differently. One of its first, and most unfortunate, acts was Prince L'vov's telegram of 5 March which was circularized to all chairmen of provincial district councils: "Whereas the Provisional Government, in the interests of internal law and order and effective defence of the State, attaches the greatest importance to ensuring that all government and public institutions continue to work without interruption, it considers it necessary to remove governors and deputy governors from office." Simultaneously, the governing of the provinces was temporarily entrusted to the chairmen of the provincial councils acting as provincial Commissars of the Provisional Government. Apart from the fact that in quite a number of provinces, where the chairman of the council had been appointed by the old government, this order simply meant the utterly senseless and unnecessary replacement of some officials by others, certainly no better, in simple rural provinces in many instances it led to complete absurdity. Not infrequently the chairman of the council was a stooge of the reactionary majority while the governor was a thoroughly acceptable person free of reactionary undertones. Very soon—almost at once, in fact—the Provisional Government was convinced that the move under consideration was an extremely rash and irresponsible bit of improvisation. But what could it do? In this instance, as in many others, it had to consider not essentials but actual practical interests—the need for revolutionary language, revolutionary demogogy, and the supposed feelings of the masses. Thus, it was to these factors that the police force was sacrificed, and a few months later its members (as well as those of the gendarmerie) naturally joined the ranks of the worst Bolshevik gangsters ("water finds its own level").

The result of this policy was the mass dismissal—and retirement, voluntary or compulsory—of a large number of high military and civilian officials. The abolition of a number of institutions and, of course, the consequent cessation of work (for example, in the State Council) brought the same result. So now there arose the question of what was to happen to this vast army of people who found themselves, as they put it in their applications, "on the rocks". A small minority deserved no attention and aroused no pity—there were, of course, among them people who were perfectly well off financially. But the overwhelming majority were people who for years had slogged away conscientiously in the Civil Service, and in some cases had reached a ripe old age and had large families to support, people who all their lives had had nothing to do with politics but had worked honestly and diligently. Among the members of the State Council were such men as N. S. Tagantsev, A. F. Koni, and other less well-known but perfectly respectable and irreproachable people.

The present masters of the situation, the Bolshevik gentlemen (whose hour, incidentally, has already struck),* have never bothered with such questions and the very idea would honestly be treated with derision by the Lenins and Trotskys. The fate of individuals means nothing to them. "When you chop down a forest, the chips must fly" is a convenient answer to everything. They do not have and have never had to face these difficulties because, of course, no one could be so naive as to expect justice and humanity. With perfectly easy consciences they kicked the whole Senate and magistracy into the street, and the tragic, hopeless situation of men who, after working all their lives now find themselves old and quite literally without a crust of bread, does not worry them in the slightest.

The Provisional Government was different. Since it did not have Jacobin fearlessness, which is frequently coupled with Jacobin unscrupulousness, the general problem concerning individuals was hard to resolve. One of the most striking examples is the dilemma of the members by appointment of the State Council. Among them were men who had not done the country any service and had been appointed for reasons of Black Hundred politics[5] in order to obtain a reactionary majority; but, as I have already mentioned, there were also professional men like Koni and Tagantsev, as well as many people for whom the State Council was the crowning of long and impeccable careers in administration or the magistracy. By law, the members of the State Council received salaries which were established in each individual case by the Supreme Authority. Similarly, pensions paid to members of the State Council were not fixed on a general basis. Very soon after the revolution, in the first weeks, in fact, when it was clear beyond all doubt that the institution of the State Council was condemned to total inactivity until the Constituent Assembly met (which of course would not retain it anyway, in any form, let alone in its present one), the Council's most honest and sensitive members felt the awkwardness of their position and the moral impossibility of receiving a large salary while doing nothing, and they raised the question of whether it was fitting to resign. In doing so, they

---

*It was possible to think so in April 1918.

had in mind (as I know for certain from my personal dealings with some of them) two considerations.

The Provisional Government did not initially abolish the State Council as an Institution. Therefore, members by appointment who found it impossible to continue enjoying the advantages of their position would have to submit their resignations, that is, they would have to take the initiative themselves. If some submitted their resignations and others did not, then clearly an absurd situation would arise: men whose first and foremost concern was to keep their salary and position would remain, while the best men would be retired. Moreover, I heard fears expressed (and I had no reason to doubt their sincerity, considering the sources from which they came) that resignations submitted by a number of people all at once or one after another might give the impression that some sort of demonstration was being made against the Provisional Government by men of authority, and this, of course, was the last thing intended. Finally, *"last not least"*, there was the question of the financial consequences for individuals, which was causing anxiety to all those who lived solely on their salaries and who could not rely either on getting another post or on private earnings. There were naturally more than a few such people, and they all were asking whether they would get pensions and of what amount. At the outset the Provisional Government assigned pensions of from 7,000 to 10,000 rubles in two cases (I think they were for V. N. Kokovtsov and A. S. Taneev, but here I may be mistaken). This was immediately discussed in political meetings outside Kshesinskaya's house (which was the headquarters of Bolshevism from the very first days). "The Provisional Government is giving pensions of thousands of rubles and wasting national wealth on servants of the old Tsarist regime." Socialist newspapers echoed the accusation. I particularly remember a nasty little article written by Mr. Goichbart (unfortunately, one of the contributors to *Pravo*) in *Novaya Zhizn'*.[6] This clamour strongly affected the Provisional Government. When finally the whole question of members of the State Council had to be faced (since it was in connexion with the State Council that the press and public were complaining about members continuing to draw salaries), the government spent two entire sessions discussing it, without being able to come to any definite decision. Some of the members of the State Council were, as they had wished, appointed to the Senate, and therefore received senatorial salaries. But the fate of the others—in my time—remained undecided. Whether any general measures were adopted later, I do not know. In this connexion I recall an episode which made me extremely sad. N. S. Tarantsev, who had been my friend for twenty years, phoned me and asked me to come and see him. He wanted to give me personally a resignation written in his own hand and an application for a pension. He was afterwards appointed to the 1st Department of the Senate and became Chairman of the Department, of which I, too, was a member, but more of this later.) As he handed me the document he could not stifle his emotion and with a sob burst out: "Yes, my dear fellow, it's very hard! After all, I've been waiting all my life for a new regime to come into being. I am the son of a peasant who registered as a merchant of the third guild to give me an education—and everything I've achieved has been solely by my own efforts. I don't owe anything to anybody, and now here I am, not wanted by anybody, going back to my original state."

Another episode belongs here. Its protagonist was a man who commanded little respect—Lipsky, the deputy and righthand man of the Governor-General of Finland—and he had the reputation of being a belligerent bully. In the revolution he was thrown out and, I remember, even arrested at the outset and deported to Finland. His political views were such that there could be no question of granting him any sort of salary. He and I were acquainted because he had been working in the State Secretariat at the end of the '90's. Now he came and saw me. He told me that his situation was quite hopeless. His wife was to undergo some major operation, he had to get her into a sanatorium, he had no place of his own in St. Petersburg—"we're crowded in with acquaintances"—and his search for private work had been in vain. He begged me to help him and lend my support in getting him allotted a senator's salary (he was a senator). What could I say to him? I realized that the matter was hopeless, but as a human being I could see that the man would simply perish. Among my drawbacks as a politician I must count a quality which prevents

31

me from saying in such circumstances: "Serves him right!" In times of revolution a politician has to be cruel and ruthless. It is difficult for someone who is organically incapable of this!

I return to my narrative.

On Saturday, 4 March N. V. Nekrasov asked me and N. I. Lazarevsky to meet him at the Ministry of Highways to deal with an assignment from the Provisional Government. It concerned the drafting of the Provisional Government's first proclamation to the country, explaining the meaning of the historical events which had taken place, stating the *profession de foi* of the government, and also defining its political programme more clearly and in greater detail than the declaration which had accompanied the government's formation. At about 2 o'clock Lazarevsky and I went to the Ministry. There we encountered feverish activity, employees running here and there and many people sitting, standing, and walking around. With some difficulty we managed to find Nekrasov chairing some meeting. We had to wait a bit, the conference finished in our presence, and Nekrasov took us through an inner corridor, out of the Ministry building, to a Minister's apartment. There, in the Minister's study, we found A. A. Dobrovol'sky, a member of the State Duma who was also, by his own wish (and, of course, by general consent), to have a hand in our work. Nekrasov explained to us the substance and aim of the proclamation and then left us alone. We got to work at once and continued until 6 or 7 o'clock in the evening. The task went smoothly and the result was a draft which I still have among my documents but which never saw the light of day.

The next day Nekrasov made a report on the draft to the Provisional Government, but, as I learned later, it met with a few partial objections. A. A. Manuilov proposed a motion to give it to F. F. Kokoshkin (who had arrived that morning from Moscow) to revise. The motion was passed. M. M. Vinaver somehow found himself involved as Kokoshkin's collaborator, and Kokoshkin left him the job of rewriting the text; this text, as Kokoshkin told me later, written entirely by Vinaver, was presented to the Provisional Government by him, Kokoshkin, and was passed without amendment. At the end of that month, Vinaver published in *Rech'* a sort of manifesto "to the Jewish people" which also began with the same words, "A mighty event has come to pass".

On the evening of the same day the first session of the Provisional Government in which I took part—or rather, at which I was present—was held in the conference chamber of the Ministry of Foreign Affairs. The second and third sessions, on 5 and 6 March, took place there, too. From 7 March onwards the sessions were transferred to the Mariinsky Palace and were held there all the time I was Head of the Secretariat and later still, until Kerensky became Prime Minister, moved to the Winter Palace (in mid-July), and transferred the sessions to the Malakhitov Hall.

These first sessions were, understandably, chaotic. Trifling matters took up a great deal of time. I remember that at practically the first session, on Saturday, Kerensky announced that he was choosing N. N. Shnitnikov as one of his deputies, and I recall that this unimportant detail made a great and extremely unfavourable impression on me at the time. It was then, for the first time as far as I was concerned, that one of that fated man's chief characteristics became manifest, namely, his total inability to understand and judge people correctly. Shnitnikov is sufficiently well known. He is a good and thoroughly honest man, but at the same time he has a narrow-minded and biased approach to any problem. His word carried no weight at all, as is well known, neither with the legal profession, the Town Duma, nor in any other sphere. And this was the man Kerensky intended to place beside him at the head of the whole legal department! Obviously he would achieve only one thing by doing this: the complete discrediting of himself and his deputy. I remember that Kerensky took quite a bit of dissuading. It should be noted, however, that his decisions, as well as being sudden and impetuous, were always irresolute and changeable. This showed itself later on a number of occasions I shall discuss in due course.

In the first few days the question of the abdicating Emperor's fate was left completely undecided. Immediately after his abdication, Nicholas II, as we know, went off to Army headquarters. At first the Provisional Government was apparently unconcerned by this. Neither on Saturday, Sunday, nor Monday, at the sessions I attended, was the need to adopt any particular measure raised for

33

discussion. The matter may, of course, have already been under discussion by then at private conferences. At any rate, I was taken completely by surprise when, on Tuesday, 7 March, I was summoned to Prince L'vov's office in the Ministry of Foreign Affairs where I found not only members of the Provisional Government, but also Vershinin, Gribunin, and, I think, Kalinin, all members of the State Duma. It was disclosed that the Provisional Government had decided to imprison Nicholas II and transfer him to Tsarskoe Selo. It has also been decided to imprison the Empress Aleksandra Fyodorovna. I was instructed to draw up an appropriate telegram in the name of General Alekseev, who was at that time the Supreme Commander's Chief of Staff. This was the Provincial Government's first decree counter-signed by me and published over my signature. . .

There can be no doubt that in the circumstances the problem of what to do with Nicholas II was a very difficult one. In more normal circumstances there would probably have been no objection to his leaving Russia for England, with whom our ties as Allies would have guaranteed that no conspiratorial attempts to put Nicholas back on the throne would be permitted. Perhaps, if the government had at once, on 3 or 4 March, shown more resourcefulness and a better management of affairs, England's consent could have been obtained, and he would have been deported at once. I do not know whether any steps toward this end were taken at the time. Apparently not. Nicholas's departure to Army headquarters complicated the situation by annoying the Executive Committee of the Soviet of Workers' and Soldiers' Deputies and gave rise accordingly to propaganda which resulted in the Provisional Government's proclamation. In actual fact, there were neither formal nor concrete grounds for declaring Nicholas II a prisoner. He had not been, formally, compelled to abdicate. To make him as Emperor answerable for particular deeds would have been absurd and contrary to the axioms of state law. In the circumstances the government obviously had a right to take steps to see that Nicholas II could not cause trouble, and it could come to an agreement with him about a fixed place of residence and decree the protection of his person. Going to England would probably have also been the most desirable course of actions for Nicholas

34

himself. Meanwhile, the warrant for arrest produced a knot that to this day has not yet been untied.* But that's not all. I am personally convinced that "kicking a man who is down", the arrest of the former emperor, contributed to inflaming seditious passions. It made the abdication look like a dethronement, since no reasons whatever were given for the arrest. Further, Nicholas II's presence in Tsarskoe Selo, a stone's throw from the capital and rebellious Kronstadt, continually alarmed and worried the Provisional Government, not because any attempts at restoration might be made, on the contrary, because of the fear that a lynching or a massacre might occur. There were times when, with the constant intensification of seditious propaganda, such fears became particularly serious.

However this may be, after Nicholas II's arrival in Tsarskoe Selo any further action was virtually ruled out; for the immediate future it became quite impossible to send the former Emperor abroad. Very much later, when Kerensky was already Prime Minister, it was decided to send the whole Imperial family to Tobol'sk, and this move was arranged in great secrecy, so much so that apparently not even all members of the Provisional Government were informed of it.

On the evening of 7 March, as I have already mentioned, the Provisional Government sat in the Mariinsky Palace for the first time. In the first weeks there were two fixed sessions a day, at 4 and at 9 o'clock. In practice the afternoon session (like the evening one) began well behind schedule and would last until 8 o'clock. The evening session always finished in the small hours. The second session was usually closed, that is, clerical staff left —only I stayed on.

This is a suitable place to discuss the outward course of events at sessions of the Provisional Government I attended during the first two months of the revolution.

As I have just said, sessions invariably began very much behind time. While waiting for them to start I would work in my office or receive the visitors who came in large numbers every day.

---

*Written in May-June 1918. A more recent (29 July 1918) footnote reads "On 16 June in Ekaterinburg this knot was finally severed".

35

I would get a message telling me when a quorum of Ministers was present. Prince L'vov, I. V. Godnev (State Inspector), and A. A. Manuilov were the most punctual. Sometimes sessions would begin with a bare quorum of Ministers who had pressing business of secondary importance. They would make their reports and obtain decisions. We did not manage at first to set a fixed agenda, and the Head of the Secretariat was not informed of matters due for report beforehand. At the first sessions, which were pretty chaotic, Ministers made their reports and one or another decision was recorded only very approximately. I managed to arrange that, as a general rule, every motion tabled ended with a draft resolution which, of course, could be amended according to the course and outcome of the debate. As for the debates at the sessions, it was decided immediately not to record them formally, and also not to register disagreements in the voting, enter personal opinions in the minutes, and so on. The underlying premise was a desire to avoid anything that might disrupt the unity of the government and its responsibility as a whole for every decision taken. The keeping of detailed minutes for every sitting, moreover, would have presented a number of considerable and almost insurmountable difficulties. The members of the Provisional Government particularly in the beginning, were inclined to view the presence of the Secretariat personnel at the sittings with a certain suspicion and mistrust. A detailed record of everything that was said would have brought protests and demands for verification, and, in the long run, considering the great number of questions reviewed at each sitting, no record would even have been completed. It must be said, incidentally, that with a few exceptions the debates at open sessions were not of much interest. Ministers were always completely exhausted when they came to the sessions. The work each one had to do was, of course, too much for normal human resources. Often very specific issues, of no concern to the majority, were handled at these sittings, and the Ministers would often be nodding off, barely listening to the reports. The excitement and passionate speeches only began at closed sessions and in sessions attended by the Liaison Commission of the Executive Committee of the Soviet of Workers' and Soldiers' Deputies.

36

Here my position was particularly irksome, and I at once felt that my role was essentially different from the part I had imagined when I took up the comparatively minor role of Head of the Secretariat. The problem was as follows.

In the Provisional Government there were personal and political friends of mine, there were casual acquaintances, and, finally, there were people I now met for the first time. Among the first group were Miliukov, Shingarev, Nekrasov, Manuilov, and, to a certain extent, Prince L'vov. The second group included Kerensky, Guchkov and Tereshchenko. The third category included Konovalov, V. N. L'vov, and I. V. Godnev. I knew M. I. Tereshchenko best of all those in the second group, but for all that our acquaintance was a purely social one. I thought of him as a brilliant young man with a very pleasant manner, a music lover and theatre-goer, an official with special functions under Telyakovsky. The jump to the Ministry of Finance in the Provisional Government had obviously been a big one, and I had difficulty in coordinating Tereshchenko's new role with my previous picture of him. But at the same time I had no reason to expect his attitude toward me to be other than completely friendly. I had known Guchkov since the days of the general congresses of the rural councils in 1905. He treated me from the outset with complete trust and courtesy. I have to say the same of the three men in the third group. I have no doubt at all that, if Kerensky had not been a member of it, I would have felt quite at ease in the milieu of the Provisional Government and would not have constrained myself to silence and to playing the part of passive observer, which I eventually found quite unbearable.

In this respect I would like now to assemble my impressions of Kerensky and others as well. I am not going to write exhaustive testimonials, which I haven't sufficient material to do anyway. But after all I did meet each of these people daily for two months; I saw them at moments of great gravity and responsibility, I was able to observe them closely, and so I assume that even my fragmentary impressions are not without some interest and may in time, when these notes of mine are used in some form or other, become part of the general mass of historical material about the Russian revolution of 1917 and its actors.

A tout seigneur tout honneur. I shall begin with Kerensky.

Seven months have passed since I last saw Kerensky, but I have no trouble in picturing his appearance. I first met him eight years ago. Our encounters were fleeting and casual; on the Nevsky, at some requiem, and the like. I was told (before his election to the State Duma) that he was gifted but not of the highest calibre. He was a bit dandified in appearance, had a clean-shaven actor's face, nearly always screwed up his eyes, and smiled in an unpleasant way which somehow left his upper teeth particularly exposed. These things taken together made him rather unattractive. In any case, not only was there nothing, either in the man himself or in what one heard about him, that gave anyone the remotest chance of forecasting what his future role would be, but also he seemed to have no notable features whatsoever. He was but one of many lawyers engaged in politics, and by no means of the first rank. He began to stand out from the mass only when he started making speeches in the State Duma. There, because of circumstances within the Party, he moved practically to the forefront and, since he was in any case head and shoulders above the nondescript colleagues around him in the Duma, since he was not a bad speaker and occasionally even a brilliant one, and since there were any number of opportunities for important speeches, it is natural that in four years he should have begun to distinguish himself and be recognized. But for all that, he never enjoyed real, substantial, generally acknowledged success. It would never have occurred to anyone to regard him as a speaker as being the equal of Maklakov or Rodichev or to compare his standing as a parliamentarian with that of Miliukov or Shingarev. In the Fourth Duma his party was unimportant and carried little weight. His position with regard to the war was basically purely Zimmerwaldian.[7] All this did anything but further the creation of any sort of aura about his name. He was aware of this, and since his vanity, like his self-conceit, is enormous and morbid, naturally there became very firmly rooted in him feelings towards his main political opponents, with which it was rather difficult to reconcile a desire to cooperate sincerely and wholeheartedly. I can certify that Miliukov was his *bête noire* in the fullest sense of the term. He never missed a chance of referring to him with spite, irony, sometimes with outright hatred. Despite his morbid and bloated vanity he could not fail to be aware that he and Miliukov were poles apart. As an intellectual force, with his vast, almost inexhaustible knowledge and breadth of mind, Miliukov was far above his colleagues in the Cabinet. Below I will try to find what in my opinion his shortcoming as a politician were. But he had an enormous advantage over Kerensky in his position with regard to the fundamental problem of war—a problem on whose solution the whole course of the revolution depended. His position was perfectly clear, well-defined, and consistent, whereas the position of "the hostage of democracy" was ambiguous, not fully articulated, and basically false. There was never the slightest trace of pettiness or conceit in Miliukov, and his personal feelings and relationships had only a most insignificant, never a determinant, effect on his political conduct. With Kerensky it was quite the reverse. He was a bundle of personal impulses.

It is difficult even to imagine the effect on Kerensky's mind of being raised to that dizzy pinnacle in the first weeks and months of the revolution. Yet in his heart he must have realized that all the admiration, all the idolization was nothing but mass hysteria, that he, Kerensky, did not have such merits and intellectual or moral qualities to justify such wild enthusiasm. But there is no doubt that from the first his whole being was shaken by the role which history had thrust upon him, a little man chosen at random, and in which it was fated for him to fail so ignominiously, leaving no mark . . .

I have just said that the idolization of Kerensky was a sign of a psychosis in Russian society. This may be an understatement. In fact, it was impossible not to wonder what the political equipment was of this man it had been decided to acknowledge as the "hero of the revolution", what he had to his credit. From this point of view it is interesting to read again in the press, now that the *"petals have fallen, the lights have gone out"*, Kerensky's *faits et gestes*, his speeches, his interviews during the eight-month period . . . If he indeed was the hero of the first months of the revolution, then that in itself is a sufficiently serious condemnation of the revolution.

Kerensky's morbid vanity, which I have mentioned, was coupled with another unpleasant trait: play-acting, a fondness for posturing, and also for any form of ostentation and pomp. His propensity to pose would show itself, I recall, even within the narrow circle of the Provisional Government where, one would have thought, it was particularly futile and absurd because everyone knew one another and no one could be deceived by anybody. One of these histrionic episodes, the clash when Miliukov mentioned the part played by German money in the Russian revolution, has been related previously.

Those who attended the so-called State Conference in Moscow's Bolshoi Theatre in August 1917 have naturally not forgotten Kerensky's speeches, the first, which opened the conference, and the last, which closed it. His effect on those who were seeing or hearing him for the first time was a depressing and negative one. His was not the calm and convincing speech of a statesman, but the veritably hysterical scream of a megalomaniac. You could sense his intense, frenzied desire to make an impression, to command respect. In the closing speech he apparently completely lost control of himself and said a lot of nonsense that had to be carefully removed from the shorthand record. Even at the very end he never understood the situation. Four or five days before the Bolshevik uprising in October, at one of our meetings in the Winter Palace, I asked him straight out if he thought a Bolshevik revolt, which everyone was talking about at the time, was possible. "I'd willingly give anything for it to happen", he replied. "And are you sure that you will be able to contain it?" "I have more forces than I need. The Bolsheviks will be crushed once and for all."

In this whole sorry story of Kerensky in power the only page which might modify the general opinion of him is his role in our last offensive (on 18 June). In my speech at the Moscow conference I possibly exaggerated this role. But there is no doubt that in this instance Kerensky showed spirit and a flash of patriotic enthusiasm, too late, alas!

Kerensky's attitude toward the Executive Committee of the Soviet of Workers' and Soldiers' Deputies was extremely curious. He honestly thought that the Provisional Government had absolute power and that the Executive Committee had no right to interfere in its work. Steklov-Nakhamkes, who during the first month was the Executive Committee's spokesman at sessions of the Provisional Government and Liaison Commission, was treated with hostility and contempt by him. Often after the meeting, or in asides during it, Kerensky would express indignation at Prince L'vov's excessive leniency with Steklov. But Kerensky himself definitely avoided arguing with Steklov, and he never once attempted to defend the position of the Provisional Government. He somehow kept changing tack and, as "the hostage of democracy", was always trying to preserve some special position of his own—a fundamentally false position which often embarrassed the Provisional Government.

My personal relationship with Kerensky had several stages. In the beginning, when I accepted the post of Head of the Secretariat, he was very suspicious of me. He apparently thought that I was reinforcing the purely Kadet element within the Provisional Government, and he tried to prevent me from playing any political role. I was perfectly well aware that any attempt on my part to join the debates, even at the closed sessions, would have met with a strong protest from Kerensky on the grounds of the Provisional Government's prerogative, and this would put me in an extremely awkward position. As a matter of fact, it was precisely Kerensky's presence which made my function so unlike what I had expected that in the early days I debated with myself whether or not I ought to keep my post. If I did not answer this question in the negative immediately, withholding my resignation until the first crisis, when after Miliukov's (and Guchkov's) resignation, Chernov, Tsereteli, Skobelev, and Peshechonov joined the ranks of the Provisional Government, it was because I was acting out of concern for a post which I wanted to leave in good order and running smoothly. Later, when Kerensky was quite sure that I harboured no personal designs, he changed his attitude. This was shown not only by offers made to me to accept a ministerial post, but also in the nature of his behaviour toward me. Finally, in the last phase, Kerensky tried, through me, to influence the Party of People's Freedom and get its support in the Council of the Russian Republic. I shall say something about this later.

After all that has been said I will hardly be suspected of bias if I, nevertheless, find myself unable to join in that stream of abuse and vilification which now always accompanies any mention of the name Kerensky. I am not denying that his part in the Russian revolution was a truly disastrous one, but this was because an inept and unconscious elemental force in the rebellion raised an insufficiently strong personality to a quite inappropriate height. The worst that can be said of Kerensky pertains to the qualities of his mind and character. We can discuss him in those words which he, with such amazing lack of moral sense and elementary tact, used about Kornilov: he loved his country "in his own way". He did in fact burn with revolutionary zeal, and at times genuine feeling broke through the actor's mask. We may recall his speech about the uprising of the serfs, his cry of despair when he realized the abyss into which Russia was being dragged by unbridled demagogy. Of course, in these speeches there was no feeling of strength or of the clear dictates of reason—they were sincere although abortive spasms. Kerensky was a captive of his own mediocre friends, of his own past. He was by nature incapable of direct, bold action and, despite his conceit and vanity, he did not have that calm and unwavering self-confidence which is the mark of strong men. There was certainly nothing heroic about him in the Carlylian sense. The blackest stain on his short-lived career is the story of his dealings with Kornilov, but I am not going to discuss that, since I know only what is common knowledge.

I shall have to return to Kerensky more than once in the course of my story. For the present I will restrict myself to what I have written and will pass on to another man on whom Russia placed immense, but unjustified hope.

I had known Prince G. E. L'vov since the first Duma. Although he was a member of the Party of People's Freedom, I do not remember that he ever actively participated in Party matters and meetings of either the branch or of the central committee. I do not think I am violating the truth if I state that he had the reputation of being a most upright and honest man who was, however, devoid of political gifts. After the dissolution of the first Duma he also was in Vyborg, but he took no part in the conferences and did not sign the proclamation.[8] I remember that he stayed in the same apartment with D. D. Protopopov and me, and he fell ill immediately on arrival, so he did not leave his room until he left Vyborg. Protopopov attributed his illness to his state of agitation. Like many of us, he was not at heart in sympathy with the proclamation, did not believe in it and thought it a mistake; but he felt that he could not prevent it because he had no acceptable and striking alternative to offer. I recall his pale, distraught face and his appearance of helplessness. Eleven years passed before I met him again. Like everybody else, I considered him an excellent organizer and set great hopes on his enormous popularity with the rural councils and the army. I have already mentioned my impression of Prince L'vov at our first meeting in the Tavrichesky Palace on the day the Provisional Government was founded. I would say that this impression was prophetic. Admittedly, in the next few days Prince L'vov was outwardly transformed, was inspired with feverish energy, and, as I initially thought at least, with faith in the possibility of establishing order in Russia.

The job of the Chairman in the first Provincial Government was certainly a very difficult one. It required great tact and the ability to control, unite, and lead men. Above all, it called for the systematic execution of a closely defined plan. Immediately following the revolution the prestige of the Provisional Government and of L'vov himself stood very high. Advantage should have been taken of this, above all to strengthen and fortify authority. It should have been realized that disruptive forces were waiting in readiness to begin their exploitation of the gigantic upheaval in the minds of the masses, a disturbance which is an inevitable consequence of any political revolution that occurs and develops as this one did. L'vov should have known how to pick energetic and competent collaborators and either devote himself entirely to the Ministry of the Interior or, once it became impossible to combine efficiently his functions as Minister of the Interior with his post as Prime Minister, to find a good deputy for the former post.

I have no wish to say anything disparaging and even less anything bad about D. M. Shchepkin or Prince S. D. Urusov, but I imagine that one could hardly expect from them what Prince L'vov himself was unable to provide. Shchepkin is a conscientious and

43

industrious worker, an excellent fellow full of energy and *bonne volonté*. But he was not a commanding figure on the basis of experience, social prestige, or his own personality; he himself knew this perfectly well, and he was hindered by this awareness in all matters he dealt with on his own. Prince Urusov was apparently at a complete loss in his new surroundings, could not find his bearings, and he felt totally out of place. After all, his government career had been spent in conditions that were fundamentally contrary to those in which he now found himself. He passed by like some pale ghost, inspired by the very best intentions, to be sure, but quite powerless to implement them. He was suited to be an assistant and an executive, but not to show determination, initiative, and originality.

The fact that the Ministry of the Interior, in other words, the whole administration and police force, remained totally disorganized, contributed in very large measure to Russia's process of disintegration. At the start there was a strange faith that everything would somehow take care of itself and would start working in a correct and organized way. Just as the revolution was idealized ("great", "bloodless"), so, too, was the populace. It was naively thought, for example, that the vast capital with its riff-raff and vicious criminal elements, ever ready to make trouble, could exist without a police force or with a shocking and absurd make shift militia, which was poorly paid and included professional thieves and convicts on the run. The nation-wide campaign against the police and gendarmerie quickly achieved a natural result. The whole organization, still functional, although haphazard and feeble, crumbled. Large numbers of police and gendarmes swelled the ranks of the Bolsheviks. In St. Petersburg and Moscow, anarchy gradually began to grow. It spread alarmingly immediately after the Bolshevik revolution. But the revolution itself was made possibe and so easy only because there was consciousness that no ready and determined authority existed to defend and preserve public order.

I would naturally be most unjust to blame Prince L'vov entirely for what happened. But one thing must be said, however severe the verdict may sound: Prince L'vov not only did nothing, but did not even attempt to do anything, to counteract the steadily spreading disintegration. He sat in the driver's seat but made no attempt to pick up the reins. In so many agonizing sessions I attended the Provisional Government's total impotence, its disharmony, the inner disagreement, and the smouldering and manifest hostility of some towards others, were revealed with inexorable clarity, and I do not recall a single occasion on which the Chairman used a tone of authority or expressed a firm and decided opinion. Prince L'vov was literally besieged from morning till night. Urgent telegrammes were constantly arriving with requests for instructions, clarifications, and pleas for the immediate implementation of top priority measures. L'vov was consulted both as head of government and as Minister of the Interior for every sort of reason, serious and trivial, received constant telephone calls, and was visited at the Ministry and at the Mariinsky Palace. I originally tried to fix a time for my daily report and for obtaining necessary instructions, but very soon I became convinced that this was quite futile, and on the rare occasions when my efforts resulted in something it all proved completely useless. I never got a firm and definite decision from him; he was usually inclined to accept the decision that I suggested to him. I would say that he was the very embodiment of inertia. I do not know whether this was a conscious policy or the result of his awareness of his own powerlessness, but it sometimes seemed as though L'vov had some mystical faith that everything would somehow work out by itself. At other times I felt that his attitude toward events was one of despair, that he was filled with an awareness of the impossibility of affecting their course, that fatalism had taken hold of him, and that he was continuing only for appearance's sake to play a part which, without any desire or aspiration on his part, had fallen to him.

Miliukov had played an active part in the election of L'vov as Chairman and in the removal of Rodzyanko, and Pavel Nikolaevich was later to tell me that he had often asked himself the agonizing question whether it would not have been better to leave L'vov alone and put in Rodzyanko, who was at any rate capable of taking resolute and bold action, had an opinion of his own, and knew how to stand his ground.

Prince L'vov's attitude to Kerensky also depressed me. It not infrequently aroused the indignation of my assistants in the Secretariat who saw it as an insufficient awareness of his dignity as Head of the Government. It often looked like timid ingratiation. Of course, personal motives were absolutely not involved here. Prince L'vov definitely had none, ambition was alien to him, and he never clung to power. I think he was profoundly happy the day he was relieved of his burden. All the more surprising, then, that he was unable to use the moral prestige he enjoyed when he came to power. It was not he who spoke with the voice of authority in the Provisional Government, but Kerensky . . .

In following a natural sequence I now must speak about Guchkov, but this I find most difficult of all.

In the first place, I had few opportunities to observe Guchkov as a member of the Provisional Government. He was absent for a considerable part of the time, away on trips to the battle front or army headquarters; in mid-April he was ill. But the main thing is that while he was War and Navy Minister he was quite indecipherable. Now, looking back on that mad period, I am inclined to think that from the beginning Guchkov felt in his soul that the game was lost and only stayed on *par acquit de conscience*. At any rate, the note of utter disillusionment and scepticism never sounded so clearly in anyone as it did in him whenever the subject of the army and navy arose. When he started to speak in his quiet, gentle voice, gazing into the distance with his slightly squinting eyes, I would be seized with horror and despair. Everything seemed doomed.

The first session wholly devoted to the situation at the front must have been on 7 March, on the evening of the day the sessions of the Provisional Government were transferred to the Mariinsky Palace. I can establish this date because at that session it was resolved to draft an appeal to the army and the populace which appeared on 10 March. I was given the job, wrote it on the following day, the 8th, it was debated at the day session on the 9th, and passed almost without amendment. For some reason it was not included in the Proceedings published by the State Secretariat and is preserved only in the Provisional Government's *Gazette* and in newspapers. I recall that at this session two points of view were expressed about the importance of the events that had taken place on our military operations. One view, officially expressed in speeches and reports, was that there existed a casual connexion between the Tsarist government's bungling of the war, on the one hand, and the revolution on the other. The outburst of protest against the incompetent and treacherous (Shtiurmer!) behaviour of this Tsarist government became concentrated, as it were, in the revolution. The revolution was to change this and establish a broader, more honest, and, therefore, more effective bond between ourselves and our Allies, the great European democracies. From this point of view the revolution could be considered a positive factor in the conduct of the war. It was assumed that commanders would be replaced, talented and energetic generals would be found, and that discipline would be quickly restored. It saddens me to have to say that my Party constantly tried to endorse this official optimism. For some people, like A. I. Shingarev, for example, the optimism survived until very late, until the Autumn of 1917. I consider that the failure to understand the real significance of the war as a factor in the revolution and an unwillingness to confront the revolution's consequences in the war both played disastrous parts in the events of 1917. I remember telling Miliukov, during one of our trips somewhere by car (this was while he was still Foreign Minister), of my conviction that a main cause of the revolution was war-weariness and a reluctance to continue fighting. Miliukov disagreed strongly. What he said was essentially: "Who knows? Perhaps it is due to the war that everything here is somehow still holding together, perhaps without the war everything would collapse." Of course, the mere realization that the war was destroying Russia would not have made a solution any easier. Neither then nor later could any Solomon have found a way of ending it without greatly injuring Russia, both morally and materially. But if it had been clearly realized in the first weeks that for Russia the war was hopelessly lost and that persevering would lead nowhere, there would have been a different approach to this important question and—who knows?— disaster might have been avoided. I do not mean that the mere fact of the revolution destroyed the army, and less than anybody am I inclined to underestimate the disastrous effect of that criminal and traitorous campaign which started at once. Least of all would I try to justify the Provisional Government's laxity and indifference toward this propaganda. But I am still firmly convinced that a successful pursuit of the war was incompatible with the tasks of the revolution inside the country and with the conditions in which these tasks had to be fulfilled. I think Guchkov realized this too. I remember that his speech at the session of 7 March, which was based entirely on the theme "as long as we've enough to keep alive", was so pervaded with despair that, when he asked me afterwards, "What is your opinion?", I replied that, if his assessment was correct, then in my view the only possible conclusion was that it was essential to make a separate peace with Germany. Guchkov, admittedly, did not agree, but he was unable to refute the conclusion. On that same memorable evening he suggested after the meeting that I accompany him to the War Minister's rooms (which Guchkov had already taken over at that time) and be present during his telephone conversation with General Alekseev. "Let's see what he's got to tell us." General Alekseev's information was extremely depressing. In the enormous confusion that occurred during the first days of the revolution he had immediately detected the portents of the coming collapse and the tremendous threat to the army. Guchkov told him the content of the proposed appeal and asked whether he thought such an appeal would be useful. Alekseev said that he did. Incidentally I may note that, at almost the same time as the appeal which I composed, a similar appeal written by the Ministry of War and also an Order of the Day appeared. They were both in the same vein and were quite ineffective.

Guchkov—and this is typical—was the first member of the Provisional Government to reach the conclusion that the task of the Provisional Government was hopeless and futile and that "they should resign". This was his subject more than once during the second half of April. He kept calling on the Provisional Government to surrender its powers and write its own epitaph, analysing the situation and forecasting the future. The Provisional Government's famous declaration of 23 April (about which I will speak later) originated in these conversations. "We must account for what we have done and explain why we cannot go on working.

We must write a sort of political testament." The declaration of 23 April, however, turned out to have a different tone and different conclusions. I think this was the last straw that made Guchkov resign from the Provisional Government.

In his two months as Minister of War Guchkov's part in the Provisional Government remained unclear. As I have already said, he was rarely at its meetings. Even more rarely would he express an opinion. He would try to bring a conciliatory note into conflicts that arose, but, in the memorable clash between Kerensky and Miliukov on the aims of the war and the problems of foreign policy, he somehow stayed in the background and gave no support to either side. Moreover, he generally seemed to remain deliberately in the background. His resignation from the Provisional Government was a surprise. I recall Nekrasov saying that the resignation was "a stab in the back". But Guchkov himself strove to prove that Prince L'vov certainly should have expected the War Minister's resignation and that he, Guchkov, had positively given notice of it.

I. V. Godnev, the State Inspector, was an extremely typical figure in the Provisional Government. I did not know him at all, even by sight, until I met him at the sessions of the Provisional Government. From constant reference to his name in Duma reports, in connexion with various legal problems and with disputes about the interpretation of the law, I had formed a picture of him as an expert on Russian law, as a man who may not have had specialized legal training yet had acquired the necessary knowledge in practice and was at home with legal problems. Furthermore, I supposed Godnev to be one of the important political figures in the State Duma. I well remember my impression when I first met him. He himself, his manner and, of course, his approach to political or legal problems were all imbued with the most simple-minded Philistinism, the grossest provincialism; everything about him reflected extreme naiveté and narrow-mindedness. There was something estimable and even touching in his veneration of the principle of legality, but because he was quite incapable of understanding the constant clashes between the new order and the unrepealed imperfections of the basic laws, he was at a loss at every turn, suffered agonizing bewilderment, and was genuinely upset. Politically he was completely neutral, and heated altercations and disagreements within the government upset him. An absolutely honest man, full of the best intentions and deserving sincere respect, as a member of the Provisional Government he was perplexity personified, and he apparently only stayed in his job because of his inertia and the lack of a suitable replacement. As soon as Kokoshkin was nominated (in July), Godnev, who had meekly sat with Tsereteli and Skobelev, then handed over his job to Kokoshkin, just as meekly and probably with relief.

The Chief Procurator of the Holy Synod, V. N. L'vov, was also, like Godnev, inspired by the very best motives and was also remarkably naive as well as incredibly off-handed, not so much in his own special affairs, but in general problems which reality daily set the Provisional Government. He always spoke with great verve and animation and invariably amused not only the government, but also the Secretariat staff.

On the subject of V. N. L'vov I must record an episode which occurred much later but which is relevant in my description of him.

It was the twenty-something of August 1917, the Tuesday of the week at the end of which Kornilov approached St. Petersburg. L'vov telephoned me in the morning and said he had important business he wanted to discuss with Miliukov as Chairman of the Central Committee and Vinaver as Deputy Chairman, but he had not managed to reach either of them (they were apparently away), and, therefore, was making this appointment to come and have a talk with me. We arranged that he would come to my house at 6 P.M. I was a bit late returning home, and, when I arrived, I found L'vov in my study. He was looking mysterious and very important. Without a word he held out to me a piece of paper on which was written more or less the following (I could not copy the text, but I remember it clearly) "The General who sat across the table from you requests you to warn the Kadet Ministers to resign on the such-and-such day of August [the date given was the one on which Kornilov's march took place, five days later; 28 August, I think; for the moment I cannot fix it definitely, but this could easily be done from the newspapers] in order to create new difficulties for the government and in the interests of their own safety."

These were a few lines in the middle of the sheet, and it was unsigned. Not understanding a thing, I asked L'vov the meaning of this puzzle and what precisely was required of me. "Just bring it to the attention of the Kadet Ministers." "But", I said, "they won't attach the slightest importance to an anonymous instruction like this." "Don't question me, I am not entitled to add anything more." "In that case, I repeat, I do not see what use I can make of your message." After a few mysterious words and half-statements, L'vov finally said that he would speak openly but asked me to give my word that what was said would remain between ourselves, "otherwise even I may be arrested". I replied that I wished to reserve the right to share what I learnt with Miliukov and Kokoshkin, and he at once agreed. Then he told me the following: "When I leave you, I am going to see Kerensky, and I am taking him an ultimatum; a revolution is being planned, and a programme for a new government with dictatorial powers has been established. Kerensky will be asked to accept this programme. If he refuses, that will be the end, and it will only remain for me, who am close to him and well disposed towards him, to try to save his life." In answer to my appeals for more precise information L'vov maintained an obstinate silence, saying that he had already talked too much as it was. As I remember, Kornilov's name was not mentioned, but L'vov certainly did say that the ultimatum was coming from army headquarters. With this the conversation ended and L'vov went to see Kerensky. As far as I can judge from what was published later, L'vov certainly did not do what he told me he planned to do in this first talk with Kerensky. He presented no ultimata (this was done at the end of the week after L'vov had been to Moscow and back), and he merely discussed various propositions and demands emanating from certain sectors. That at least is how Kerensky reported the conversation, and L'vov did not deny it. Unfortunately, I had no further occasion to encounter L'vov and to this day the whole incident is inadequately explained as far as I am concerned. I am certain of one thing. Either L'vov suddenly changed his plans on the way to the Winter Palace, or Kerensky had known for five days what was planned. I personally am inclined to accept the latter supposition. Unfortunately, at the time I am writing these lines,* I have not yet read Kerensky's book on the Kornilov affair, which embellishes it with various, very recent pieces of evidence. But if it is true that such an important mission was entrusted to V. N. L'vov, then this clearly shows that the initiators of the revolt were very bad judges of character and acted exceedingly rashly ... Miliukov later suggested that in this whole business L'vov had "got into a shocking tangle". I repeat, for me it remains a mystery. I should add that I reported our conversation that same evening to Kokoshin, as well as to other Kadet Ministers (Ol'denburg and Kartashov) whom I met almost daily at A. G. Krushchyov's flat. I remember that I asked them to observe Kerensky's behaviour at the evening session. They informed me that there had been no difference, Kerensky had behaved as he always did.

To my characterization of V. N. L'vov I can add one more note: when Miliukov twice acquainted the Provisional Government with out "secret" treaties, nothing could have been more genuine, more ingenious, more naive than L'vov's indignation. He called them gangsterish and crooked and apparently argued that we should immediately renounce them. He was particularly annoyed about Italy and the "annexations" (the world had not yet become popular) which she reserved for herself. With the same ingenuousness he would speak of the "idiots and scoundrels" sitting in the Synod. An almost comic despair pervaded his reports. There is no doubt that V. N. L'vov had more than one virtue: he was not a political schemer, and he threw himself heart and soul into his task of improving the administration of the Church at the highest levels. Unfortunately, this task was far beyond him. Like Godnev, when his seat required for another he surrendered it without a murmur. In spite of all the energy he generated in his five months as Chief Procurator, I do not know whether his work left even a slight mark in the "Department of the Orthodox Church".

I have already spoken of my surprise at finding that M. I. Tereshchenko was Minister of Finance. At first I even refused to believe that this could be that brilliant young man who a few years

---

*The end of July 1918.

before had appeared on the St. Petersburg scene, made his way into theatrical circles, become well known as a keen music-lover and patron of the arts, and at the outbreak of war, thanks to his enormous wealth and connexions, became a prominent figure in the Red Cross. Later he had been at the head of the Kiev War Industries Committee and at a congress held in St. Petersburg he had made what could be called the speech of a "repentant capitalist". To my knowledge, this was his only public speech. I did not know that he was apparently close to Guchkov and Nekrasov and was liked by Rodzyanko. To this day I do not know for certain who nominated him. I heard that he had obstinately refused nomination. He is remembered mainly today as a man who held the post of Foreign Minister for six months, from the beginning of May until the end of October when the Provisional Government was overthrown. As Minister of Finance, in his two months at that post, he seemed to have made no perceptible mark whatsoever. He was chiefly concerned with issuing the famous Freedom Loan. I remember that his reports to the Provisional Government were always very clear and not verbose but, on the contrary, very concise and beautifully expounded. In fact, I am not going to pass judgment on his qualities as Minister for Finance. He was excellent at getting a surface grasp of things, knew how to find his way about, and how to converse with people, saying just what his listener wanted to hear and falling in with the other man's views. As Foreign Minister he endeavoured to follow Miliukov's policy, but in such a way as to avoid trouble from the Soviet of Workers' Deputies. He wanted to fool everybody and for a time he succeeded. . . In September 1917 the Socialists grew disappointed with him and expected nothing further from him, but Sukhanov-Gimner had much earlier begun a campaign against him in *Novaya Zhizn'*. During July and August he, Nekrasov, and Kerensky comprised a triumvirate which formulated the whole policy of the Provincial Government and in this capacity he bears responsibility for the weakness, duplicity, unscrupulousness, and futility of that policy, which constantly veered and sought compromises just when only the rejection of compromise, resoluteness, and certainty could provide the one solution. In October, from the moment the Council of the Russian Republic

53

was formed, Tereshchenko ostentatiously broke with the Socialists. By accident I witnessed his stormy confrontation with Kerensky at which he insisted that the Provisional Government release him from the Foreign Ministry portfolio, and at this time he indicated that I was the one to be his successor. But it was too late. M. I. Tereshchenko met a sad fate. He wanted to win everybody's sympathy, to be generally liked. Nevertheless, he did not put down firm roots anywhere, neither in any social circle, nor in any political group, and nobody valued him or had a high opinion of him. *Ce n'était pas un caractère.* What is remarkable is that our Allies' diplomatic representatives liked Tereshchenko much more than Miliukov. His *souplesse*, his good manners, his lack of firm convictions or well-devised plans, and his complete dilettantism in matters of foreign policy made him in the circumstances a man eminently suited to conversation, and during the existence of the Provisional Government foreign policy never got beyond conversation.

Toward the end of the Provisional Government's rule, after N. V. Nekrasov's resignation, Tereshchenko conceived a burning hatred for the Socialists. This was a change of position. I have reason to believe that his change of heart was influenced by the Kornilov affair. I do not know Tereshchenko's attitude as this affair was developing, but he was greatly shocked by the suicide of Krymov,[9] with whom he had been friendly. He found the "Socialist Front" persecution of Kornilov most distressing and distasteful, and it aroused his indignation; he told me so himself. I think it was also because of this that a certain coolness developed between him and Kerensky. At the same time, he believed, or wanted to believe, right up to the very last that it was possible to regenerate the Army and restore the front line. He and I discussed this in September or October 1917. He stated categorically that Alekseev would have a new army trained by the spring of 1918. When the Provisional Government's last Minister for War, General Verkhovsky, stated bluntly in the War Commission of the Council of the Republic that Russia could not go on fighting, Tereshchenko made a sharp rejoinder. His clash with Verkhovsky in the Commission was one of the most memorable incidents during the last days of the Provisional Government.

54

Alas, it must be admitted that Verkhovsky was in fact right . . .

In sum, I would say that Tereshchenko, despite his outstanding ability and undoubted *bonne volonté*, was not, and could not be, equal to the political task that fell to him. The job was just as far beyond him as it was beyond most of the other Ministers. He was as incapable as they of "saving Russia". And between March and October 1917 Russia needed quite literally to be saved.

Finally, among the members of the Provisional Government whom I hardly knew was A. I. Konovalov, the Minister of Trade and Industry. I first met him at the Tavrichesky Palace in the early days of the revolution, and I observed him during my two months as Head of the Secretariat of the Provisional Government. After that I completely lost sight of him and did not come across him again until he was Deputy Chairman in the last Provisional Government.

Here is a man of whom I could say nothing unfavourable by way of a personal appraisal. Both as Minister of Trade and later, when for his sins he considered it his patriotic duty to heed Kerensky's urgent request, and again entered the Cabinet, accepting, moreover, the very responsible and onerous job of being Kerensky's deputy, he was constantly martyred, and he suffered greatly. I do not think he believed for one moment that a favourable outcome was possible. As Minister of Trade he could see clearly and at close hand our disastrous path toward economic collapse. Later, as Deputy Chairman, he encountered all Kerensky's bad features. At the same time, Konovalov was already perfectly well aware in October 1917 that for Russia the war was over. At this time (or earlier, in September after the formation of the last Cabinet) a conference was held in Prince Grigorij Nikolaevich Trubetskoy's apartments (in the Sergievskaya, in Weiner's house, where we had lived in the Winter of 1906-7). Neratov, Baron Nol'de, Rodzyanko, Savich, Maklakov, M. Stakhovich, Struve, Tret'yakov, Konolalov, and I were present (I think I have named everybody; Miliukov was in the Crimea where he had gone after the Kornilov affair) to discuss whether it was possible and right to direct Russia's future policy toward a general peace. Konovalov decidedly supported the view of Baron Nol'de who, in a well-considered and shrewd report, argued that precisely such a course was essential. Unfortunately, all this was too late anyway . . .

But all these recollections relate to Konovalov's second period in office. I do not remember that he played a notable role in the first Provisional Government. He spent most of the time, I think, complaining—complaining primarily that the Provisional Government was insufficiently concerned with the industrial havoc that was growing not daily but hourly due to the excessive and increasing demands of the workers. He was never eloquent, and spoke very simply and sincerely, almost ingenuously, but I think that a note of panic could be heard in his speeches to the Provisional Government. In private coversations he would often raise his complaints as though seeking approval and moral support. How Konovalov could have entered the Provisional Government a second time with Kerensky as Chairman is for me an unsolved mystery. Apparently he thought it his patriotic duty not to refuse and imagined it possible to hang on until the Constituent Assembly. At the time that mirage, the Constituent Assembly, aroused in many minds quite unrealizable hopes. In a separate place I will discuss the importance of the idea of a Constituent Assembly to the Provisional Government . . .

I met A. I. Konovalov for the last time in tragic circumstances, on the day the Provisional Government was overthrown, 26 October. I shall also have to talk about that day in due course.

Until now I have touched upon the character and role of those men in the Provisional Government who were not of the same Party as myself. I made the acquaintance of some for the first time in the Provisional Government. Now it remains for me to talk about four Kadet Ministers, Miliukov, Shingarev, Nekrasov and Manuilov, whom I had known for a long time, although I was on close personal terms only with Miliukov.

The one I knew least well was Manuilov. This is, of course, because Manuilov is a Muscovite and never took a particularly active part in the meetings of the Central Committee, and outside those meetings I hardly ever met him. I must say that during the two months I was working for the Provisional Government Manuilov remained constantly in the background. Very rarely, if at all, did he participate in the heated political debates that went on in the closed sessions. I recall that in the chief controversy of the first month about foreign policy and the aims of the war, Manuilov gave very feeble support to Miliukov; in fact I would even say that he gave no support at all. On the other hand, a sense of the hopelessness of the Provisional Government's task somehow took hold of Manuilov before it did others, and he said more often and earlier than others that the Provisional Government should resign because the restriction and constant obstruction by the Soviet of Workers' Deputies made it impossible to work. As Minister of Education he was not as authoritative as might have been expected. This may well not have been his fault, that is, not the fault of his personal qualities. In other, more normal circumstances, these qualifications would have made him an exemplary Minister of Education, since there can be no doubt of his breadth of view, great knowledge, and general virtues as a politician and administrator. But the fact is, his was not a combative nature, he was no fighter. Even very early on his main method of fighting had been to hand in his resignation. This may have been all right under Kasso, but at this particular moment something else was required. Manuilov might have been perfectly fitted for the post of Minister of Agriculture, although I imagine that by temperament and constitution he was actually not the man suited to this particular revolutionary moment. He did not impress anybody. Added to this, his balanced disposition as an intellectual European was heartily disturbed by the atmosphere of unbridled, demagogic radicalism. I remember Manuilov's despair at the time of the Teachers' Congress. It was in the field of education that our Jacobin radicalism was particularly marked, and if eventually the educators got Mr. Lunacharsky as their leader, then we can properly say: *"Tu l'as voulu, Georges Dandin."* Of all the Ministers Manuilov received the worst press. He was attacked by the Right and the Left: By the Right for not taking action and for apathy in the face of the growing wave of revolution, and for the Spelling Reform (which, as we know, had nothing to do with him; the Academy of Sciences has that horror on its conscience); and by the Left for bureaucracy, for encouraging red-tape, and for appointing officials of the old regime. Gerasimov's appointment was a cause of particular irritation. Manuilov did not know how to defend himself and ward off attack. He would get depressed and give way to despair. As a matter of fact, he may have been quite right in judging the situation to be hopeless. But even so he should have acted differently, more decisively, I would even say, more demonstratively. Despite his merits he remained a rather dim figure, and if his appointment was welcomed, his resignation and the appointment of S. F. Ol'denburg as his replacement not only caused no regret, but was favourably received even in circles sympathetic to him.

I find it most difficult to discuss Nekrasov. At the beginning of my essay I mentioned that, as the result of my prolonged absence from the Central Committee, I was very ill-informed about the personal relationships which had formed there and in the State Duma. It was only long after I had become Head of the Secretariat of the Provisional Government that a talk with A. I. Shingarev opened my eyes. He told me about the "underground war" which Nekrasov was waging against Miliukov. Only then did I understand the behaviour of Nekrasov, whom, until then, I had by force of habit looked on as one of Miliukov's most devoted friends. But even so I still did not quite grasp Nekrasov's aim. However, each day provided clearer and clearer indications that he was leaning toward the Socialists, drawing closer to Kerensky with whom he had greater and greater influence; and more often he sang the same tune. All the same, I do not know Nekrasov intimately enough to judge him with confidence; yet I fear that, while he was in the government, he was guided first and foremost by motives of ambition. He sought to play the leading role, and he achieved his aim, but only to the extent that he inspired Kerensky to behave shamefully in the Kornilov affair, following which he left the scene with a damaged political reputation, abandoned by all his former friends (even such devoted and intimate friends as I. P. Demidov) and nicknamed the "evil genius of the Russian revolution". Nevertheless, I am firmly convinced that Nekrasov is one of the few outstanding men to have emerged in the political arena in recent years. His business capabilities are great, he knows how to find his bearings, his outlook is broad, and he is quick to grasp practical questions. An intelligent, astute, eloquent man, he knows how to appear frank and ingenuous when necessary. But apparently his ethical qualities (I am, of course, speaking of his social and political, not personal qualities) were not comparable to his intellectual qualities. I am quite prepared to believe that essentially he was striving for the victory of those ideas which united him with his fellow party members. But to achieve this victory he chose a tortuous path that ended in a blind-alley. I imagine that at this moment (1918) he must be a very unhappy man and that his political career is finally over. He will never again inspire confidence in anybody, and confidence is after all absolutely essential for a politician. Once duplicity is seen it is never forgotten. It was precisely an impression of duplicity, of a mask hiding his true face, that Nekrasov gave. It was particularly noticeable because his seeming kindness was so disarming. A "*faux bonhomme*" as the French so neatly put it, is perhaps the most unpleasant personality pattern of man in general and among politicians in particular.

If the Kadet element in the Provisional Government was personified above all in Miliukov, then one must say that only Shingarev gave the party his absolute whole-hearted and unflagging support and assistance.

As I write these lines, more than six months have elapsed since Shingarev's tragic death, and yet even in these notes it is somehow difficult to speak about the dead man with complete freedom. He paid far too high a price for the great exploit of his life. Nevertheless, I will try in this case, too, to write the truth as I see it. The truth here is that throughout his life Shingarev remained essentially what he would have been in more normal circumstances: a provincial Russian intellectual, a representative of the third estate, very capable and industrious, warm-hearted and high-minded, moved by the purest motives, personally most charming and likeable, but ultimately suited to be active not at the State but at Provincial or District level. He became a financier purely by chance. Thanks to his ability and diligence he made himself so at home in finance that he could speak in opposition in the Duma and be successful. But he was quite unable to impress real experts, either theorists or practical men. His dilettantism, his poor training, and the limitations of his perspective were too obvious. His virtues and amazing fascination made him one of the most popular and best-liked members in the Duma. The press fawned upon him. The government was very attentive to his views. Large numbers of people consulted him daily for all sorts of reasons. His popularity within the Party was enormous. If it fell short of Miliukov's, then this perhaps was so only in that Miliukov stood higher as an intellectual force, as spiritual leader and guide, and as a statesman, but Shingarev was better loved, particularly in the provinces where his speeches, addresses, and lectures were always a great success. The middle classes had a greater spiritual affinity with Shingarev than with Miliukov. He was closer to them, more like one of them. As a speaker Shingarev was naturally not comparable to Maklakov and Rodichev (when the latter was at his best). He rarely gave a feeling of strength. There was no imagery, no sparkle in his speeches. He was quite unable to rivet attention, to stir emotions, to shock. What is more, one did not sense in these speeches, which were always very prolix as well, that scope of ideas and knowledge that was so clearly felt when Miliukov spoke. He was no spell-binder like Maklakov, he did not move and excite like Rodichev, but he spoke effortlessly and fluently, his train of thought was always very clear and easy to follow, in debate he was quite often resourceful and witty, and his voice and manner were captivating. Although one could stop listening to him without any regrets, one was almost never with the feeling that he had not been worth listening to. In *The Possessed* Dostoevsky says that one cannot listen to one speaker for more than twenty minutes. This is definitely not true of our provincial audiences. They love verbosity and regard their boredom as proof of the seriousness and importance of the speech or lecture, not without reason have such dull mediocrities as Gredeskul always had enormous success in the provinces.

By the end of the Fourth Duma Shingarev's standing was very high. To any objective observer it was obvious that his self-conceit and self-confidence had increased, especially after members of the Duma made their trip abroad in the spring of 1916. One had the impression that Shingarev was feeling slightly giddy from the height to which he, a modest country doctor, had been elevated, not by chance or by outside help, but by his own efforts. Had it not been for the State Duma, Shingarev would have lived the upright and respectable life of an educated local public figure, a selfless toiler. The State Duma brought him to the forefront and prepared one to accept him as one of the most obvious candidates for Ministerial rank as soon as the old regime fell. He was then submerged in a vast amount of work that was too much for any one man alone. He did not trust or rely on anybody very much. He wanted to deal with everything himself, and this was physically impossible. He probably worked 15 to 18 hours a day, completely overtaxed himself, and very soon lost his flair and good spirits. He often spoke at the Provisional Government's sittings, but it was precisely there that his powers proved inadequate. At these sessions, too, he thought he was on the platform in the State Duma, spoke at length and was terribly verbose, and exhausted himself and everybody else. But the worst insult one could render him was to say: "Andrei Ivanych, can't you make it a bit shorter?" In such instances he would reply: "I don't need to speak at all", thereby compelling you to persuade him to . . . His attitude to Kerensky and the whole Socialist morass was unfavourable and hostile, yet he was not only unable to give them a good fight; on the contrary, with such measures as the setting up of Land Committees and transferring uncultivated estate lands to them as well as (while he was Minister of Finance) the totally unjustifiable and completely absurd raising of his income tax, he played into the hands of the Socialists, making himself many implacable enemies among landowners and the propertied classes generally. He himself had little faith in his own law introducing a grain monopoly. Incidentally, the prices fixed by the law were constantly being changed right up to the last minute; in the long run, apparently, many of them had to be written off as failures. In matters of general and foreign policy Shingarev was unfailingly on Miliukov's side, but I cannot remember that he made any powerful or brilliant speeches. After he finally resigned from the Provisional Government, Shingarev became extremely peevish and acrimonious—I am inclined to say embittered. It was difficult to debate with him in the Central Committee because he received any argument very badly, as though it were directed against him personally. Sometimes his tongue had a very rough edge to it. Presumably, the personal misfortunes he suffered during this period (the death of his wife) seriously affected his already over-strained nerves. He became difficult, and maintained his former manner and attitude toward only a few (among whom I was one). N. I. Lazarevsky told me it was very difficult to work with Shingarev. He was, as Lazarevsky put it, singularly suspicious and mistrustful of everybody around him with the exception of a small circle of intimates he personally chose. His death in January 1918 is one of the most tragic and at the same time most senseless episodes in the bloody history of Bolshevism.

As I have already had occasion to say before, there is no doubt that the most important intellectual and political figure in the first Provisional Government was Miliukov. I regard him generally as a most remarkable Russian, and I would like to try to give a more detailed picture of him.

I have often had occasion to hear Miliukov speak: in the Central Committee, at party congresses and gatherings, at meetings and public lectures, in State institutions. His qualities as a speaker are closely related to his personality. He is most successful whenever he has to make a controversial analysis of some situation. He is a master of irony and sarcasm. His magnificent exposés, with their captivating logic and clarity, can crush an opponent. At political meetings no speaker from opposing parties has ever managed to confuse him or put him off his stride. The outward form of his speech does not concern him. It has no imagery, no structural beauty. But it also never has what the French call *du remplissage*. If he tends toward prolixity in his speeches and in his writings, it is only because he must express his thought in exhaustive detail. Here, too, his complete disregard of the setting, coupled with his unusual indefatigability, shows itself. When his turn comes, late at night, after a full day of heated debate, he unhurriedly and methodically begins his speech and is at once oblivious to all incidental considerations; his listeners' weariness has nothing to do with him; he pays no attention to the fact that they may simply be unable to follow the trend of his thoughts. In his newspaper articles he does not care either about purely journalistic considerations. If he needs two hundred lines, he writes two hundred lines, but if his ideas and his argument will not fit into them, he does not care if his editorial spreads over three columns.

Like many others, Miliukov, too, is living and has lived at a time in history unsuited to his personal talents. Fate so willed it that Miliukov should take office just when what was needed was a strong, unwavering government that would not hesitate to act resolutely, when the highest degree of unity and solidarity among members of the government and their mutual trust were required. He found himself at the head of the government department that directs foreign policy just when a serious disagreement about the prerequisites of this policy existed between himself and those who followed the ideas of Kerensky. I have personally heard Kerensky align himself, if not directly with the Zimmerwaldians, at least with elements intellectually allied to them. Both in the press and on the platform of the State Duma, Miliukov carried on a stubborn fight with the Zimmerwaldian outlook from the beginning. He was absolutely alien and hostile to the idea of peace without annexation and indemnity. He considered that it would be absurd and simply criminal of us to renounce the "greatest prize of the war" (as Grey called Constantinople and the Straits) for the sake of the humanitarian and cosmopolitan ideas of international Socialism. But most importantly, he believed that this prize had not really slipped from our grasp. This belief is related to his general views on the revolution's significance for the war. This is the very key to the tragedy which Russia has suffered.

Miliukov's attitude to the imminent threat of war in June and July 1914 is well known. He wrote that it was a grim and terrible danger fraught with enormous disasters. Of course, neither he nor any other politician realized or could realize what the war would make of Europe and what it would do to Russia. Above all, no man living would have believed, if he had been told in 1914, that boys then thirteen years old would be participating in the war, or that four years hence the war would be raging at its height and that even then there would be little hope of an approaching conclusion. Nevertheless, Miliukov saw clearly, firstly, the terrible risk for Russia entailed in the declaration of war in Europe, and secondly, how unlikely it was that the "historical government", whose rule in Russia had proved so hopelessly and immeasurably incompetent and inconsistent during peacetime, would rise to its allotted task. For this reason, in a series of articles in *Rech'*, Miliukov appealed with all the force of his conviction for cool-headedness, self-control, and moderation. Everybody also knows how maliciously he was attacked by our militant, nationalistic press, headed by *Novoe Vremya*.[10] The question was "intervention in defence of Serbia", and, since Miliukov was regarded as a "Bulgarophile" and, consequently, a "Serbophobe", hostility to "little Serbia" and indifference to Russia's international prestige were read into his speeches or attributed to him. A furious campaign was initiated which resulted in the closing of *Rech'* (admittedly, only for a short time) on the day war was declared. War broke out, and at once Miliukov adopted a perfectly well-defined attitude toward it. Both in the State Duma and in the party as well as in *Rech'*, he carried on an energetic campaign to stimulate enthusiasm for the war. The slogan "War until Victory" belongs to a later period, but its roots are in earlier days. When it transpired that England was joining France and Russia, the conviction which definitely prevailed was that the war would soon be over and Germany defeated. I remember only too well being told quite seriously in August or September by Count P. N. Ignat'ev (an intimate friend of mine since my student days), whom I had met for dinner in a restaurant and who apparently really believed that such a plan could be successfully carried out, that Rennenkampf was marching straight for Berlin, by-passing strongholds and leaving behind covering detachments, and that he swore he would be in Berlin within two months. I also remember writing for the first time from Staraya Russa, where my battalion was gathering, to A. I. Kaminko, saying that I was more convinced each day of the enormity of the undertaking and of the impossibility of any quick conclusion. But our early successes in East Prussia and then in Galicia considerably strengthened our hopes, and only the terrible surprises during the second half of the winter of 1914-15 showed how rash we had been. At the same time, the State Duma's tactics toward the government suddenly changed. Support for the Cabinet was the *mot d'ordre* in the autumn of 1914, something like the French *Union Sacre*. But by the spring of 1915 it had emerged that to support Sukhomlinov, Maklakov, and Shcheglovitov would lead Russia knowingly to defeat and disaster. So the struggle began. The course of this struggle and the changes of fortune are well known. Well known, too, is the part played by Miliukov, and so, at the very outset the tragic misunderstanding which influenced the course of the Russian revolution and led Russia to ruin was revealed.

What was the point of the struggle? Obviously, first and foremost and *ex professo*, so to speak, it was to establish in Russia a government capable of correcting the mistakes and blunders which had already been made, and of properly organizing supplies and reinforcements for the Army. In other words, the purpose of the struggle was to form a government that could conduct a better and more efficient war. Meanwhile, all the reshuffling in the government began to look more and more like some senseless game of ministerial leapfrog. Decent and effective people like Prince Shcherbatov and Polivanov were not long at their posts. Their places were taken either by impecunious mediocrities like General Shuvaev or by sinister figures like Aleksei Khvostov and, later, Shtiurmer. A smell of folly and death hung in the air. Behind the scenes Rasputin, Prince Andronnikov, and other rogues were running the show. From the outbreak of war until the disaster which befell him in the early days of March 1917, the Tsar did not realize the fatal significance of what was happening. Those who experienced the winters of 1915-16 and 1916-17 in St. Petersburg well remember how a sense of some inevitable catastrophe grew daily. I was informed that as early as 1914, at a meeting of the Central Committee of the Kadet Party immediately after the outbreak of war (I was then already in Staraya Russa), Rodichev had exclaimed: "Do you really think we can win with these fools?" It gradually became clear that the folly of our home policy, the shady atmosphere of irresponsible recklessness, and total disregard of the country's interests by a throne which was completely estranged from the country and occupied by a weak, worthless hypocrite, must all lead either to a separate peace or to a revolution. Progressive public opinion in Russia, which had long since lost faith in Nicholas II, gradually realized that, as Kokoshkin eloquently put it in his speech on the republic and monarchy, one could not at the same time be both for the Tsar and for Russia, that to be for the Tsar meant to be against Russia.

On 1 November 1916, Miliukov made his famous speech, "Stupidity or Treason?" Though aimed directly at Shtiurmer, this speech actually had targets in much higher places. The name of the Empress, Aleksandra Fyodorovna, was openly mentioned. Everybody remembers the tremendous impression it made, but probably not everybody realized the consequences it would have. Only much later, after the revolution, was it commonly stated, particularly by Miliukov's friends, that the beginning of the Russian revolution dated from the speech of 1 November. Miliukov himself, I believe, took a different view. He was fighting for a Cabinet which would enjoy public confidence, to isolate the Tsar and make him innocuous (when once it transpired that the Tsar in no way and under no circumstances could be a help in governing the country or running the war), to make it possible for progressive forces to take an active and responsible part in the government's work. I think it was during the winter of 1916-17 that Miliukov realized the need for definite action, particularly with reference to Nicholas II. But I suppose that he saw it, as many others did, rather like an eighteenth-century palace revolution and did not realize how great the coming shocks would be. On the other hand, Miliukov's standpoint with regard to the war became more and more definite, more closely linked with our Allies, and England in particular, and more implacable toward Germany. I well remember his effect on me and a few close friends who had met for dinner at I. V. Gessen's house on the day a telegram brought news of Germany's first peace proposals. For us this was news of staggering importance, chiefly because it gave hope, even though feeble and very distant, that peace might be possible. It was mainly from that angle that we were judging it. Immediately Miliukov doused our hopes with ice-cold water. Calmly and even happily he declared that the German proposals were important only insofar as they provided evidence of Germany's difficult situation, that only in this sense should they be understood and welcomed, but that the only possible answer was a categorical rejection of them in the strongest terms. Clearly, such an attitude on Miliukov's part was strictly dictated by a profound belief in "ultimate victory" and in Russia's ability to conclude the war so as to enjoy the fruits of victory. In a recent letter Miliukov himself has referred to the mood prevailing in Europe's ruling circles as "war fever". I think that this fever has been the basis of all international policy since the outbreak of the war. Italy, then Rumania, and last of all, America entered the war not from a correct understanding of their legal national interests, and even less were motives of political ethics influential; it was simply a fever of the sort which takes hold of anyone who watches a mighty game with colossal stakes and who knows that it up to him to get into the game and ensure himself a share of the spoils. The famous treaties with Italy and Rumania are nothing but a division of the spoils. Of course, the booty was sought not for personal but for national interests. Naturally Miliukov, too, in grabbing at and clinging tenaciously to the promise of Constantinople and the Straits, was thinking only of Russia's good. But in the long run aggression can always be justified by a concern for a country's good. Miliukov's real attitude toward the war was always much closer to Romain Rolland's than to Barres' and *"l'Action Française"*. The ideas and points of view which took hold of Miliukov from 1914 to 1917 were not deeply held; he himself even felt they were alien to him, and his escape from them must have seemed to him to be a "spiritual liberation". As I imagine it, this liberation was a return to an objectivity which is in keeping with the fundamental concepts of justice and humanity and with the rejection of bloodshed and violence, rather than with any immediate practical political aim.

However this may be, it is very clear from what I have said that the conflicts which were to arise both within the Provisional Government and between the government and the elements around it most deeply involved in the revolutionary movement were inevitable. The most influential figure in the Provisional Government proved to be "the hostage of democracy", Kerensky. If on the day the Provisional Government was formed it had occurred to anyone to nominate Kerensky as Minister of War, I think even Kerensky, in spite of his infinite aplomb, would have been embarrassed. Everybody else would have taken the nomination as a jibe, a silly joke. Nevertheless, within two months Kerensky was the "providential" Minister of War. The same thing applies, indeed even more so, to the post of Supreme Commander. I remember a lengthy sitting in the Mariinsky Palace devoted to debating and settling the question of whom to appoint to the post, Alekseev (the former Chief of Staff of the Supreme Commander at the time) or Brusilov. The latter was particularly strongly supported by Rodzyanko. I can imagine the effect under the circumstances if Kerensky had been nominated. This, too, certainly would have been simply regarded as a joke in bad taste. Yet once again it came true a few months later. I do not think there is any better measure of the speed with which the Zimmerwaldian outlook gained the upper hand, with the consequent destruction of our army, than these two appointments. But, practically speaking, the germ of future decay was already inherent in the fact that, when the Provisional Government was formed, the fundamental question, that of the war, was passed over; otherwise how was it possible to include both Miliukov and Kerensky, whose views were sufficiently well known from his speeches in the State Duma, in one government?

It should be noted that during the first days and even weeks of the Provisional Government foreign policy in relation to the war was somehow not discussed. The unnoticed but grave inner contradiction of the revolution was that it came as a result of a military uprising and so had to lead to a breakdown of discipline and disintegration (first in the St. Petersburg garrison, and then, as this garrison became a hot-bed of Bolshevism and a breeding-ground of infection, the disintegration spread further); but according to the official ideology, the revolution was supposed to increase our military might, since our troops henceforth would be fighting for a liberated Russia, not for a hated autocratic regime. We know that in the early days a lot of simple-minded people thought (and even wrote in the newspapers) that Germany had been greatly upset by the patriotic impulse of the Russian revolution; Germany, it was said, had at first placed great hopes on the revolution but now she would discover that a "cognizant" Russian army, which had won its freedom, would be more terrible to deal with. . . and more in that vein. I don't know whether anybody really believed such nonsense, but, I repeat, it was not only devel-

68

oped in the newspapers, but it was also repeatedly and persistently declared officially (for example, at Embassy receptions and at receptions of the numerous military deputations which began to arrive at the end of March). In the meantime, gradually and imperceptibly the slogan "War until final victory" was undermined by another, "Peace without annexations and indemnities". Little by little complaints that Miliukov was quite independently conducting a foreign policy of his own were heard within the Provisional Government. The rift in the government began to show, but at first rather vaguely and imperceptibly. If I am not mistaken, the matter came to a head after an interview with Miliukov on the problems of the war appeared in the press (in the 23 March issue of *Rech'*), and about a week later the notorious appeal of the Soviet of Workers' and Soldiers' Deputies to the peoples of the whole world was published (on 14 March), an appeal in which the leaders of the Executive Committee showed their true colours for the first time. It is hard to imagine a greater contrast than these two documents provide. I don't know whether it was due to the influence of his friends or whether it was spontaneous, but Kerensky was greatly agitated by the Miliukov interview. He had apparently just returned from Moscow. I clearly remember that he brought the issue of *Rech'* with him to the meeting, and, before Miliukov arrived, in his inimitable way he guffawed unnaturally, drummed his fingers on the newspaper, and muttered to himself, "No, no, this stunt won't do". When the subject was raised Miliukov stated that his interview had been intended to countervail an interview with Kerensky which had been printed, if I'm not mistaken, in a Moscow newspaper. I do not remember whether it was at this or a later meeting that Kerensky tried in strong language to persuade Miliukov that if under "Tsarism" (one of those foul bits of revolutionary jargon but alien to the spirit of the Russian language) the Foreign Minister could not and should not have any policy but the policy of the Emperor, so now the Foreign Minister could not have his own policy but only that of the Provisional Government. "We are for you, your Majesty the Emperor." Miliukov, outwardly calm but inwardly agitated, answered approximately as follows: "I have considered and still consider that the policy I am following is the policy of the Provisional

Government. If I am wrong, then let me be told so straight out. I demand a definite answer and according to this answer I shall know what I am to do in future." Here was a direct and definite challenge, and this time Kerensky shirked it. In the person of Prince L'vov the Provisional Government attested that Miliukov was following not his own independent policy but a policy in conformity with the view and plans of the Provisional Government. A way out of this awkward situation was found by passing a motion that in future no personal political interviews should be granted. At the same time the wish was expressed that Miliukov make a detailed report with a view to fully acquainting the Provisional Government with all aspects of the international situation and in particular, with all the famous "secret treaties". This was done as early as the first half of April, but even before that, at the end of March, the Provisional Government's declaration on the problems of the war was published.

The initiative for this declaration came from Tsereteli. About the middle of March he returned from exile, and early in the last week of the month he appeared in the Liaison Commission, replacing Steklov. From the very start, probably at the first session he took part in, he urgently advocated that a solemn declaration should be made without delay to the army and the people; should contain, firstly, a definite break with imperialistic aims, and secondly, an assurance that steps would be taken immediately toward a general peace. He argued that, if the Provisional Government would make such a declaration, the army's morale would rise to unprecedented heights, and he and those of like mind would be able, with complete confidence and assured of success, to rally the army behind the Provisional Government, which would thereby acquire enormous moral strength. "Say it", he said, "and everybody will be behind you as one man." I remember that at the time his tone and manner were winningly persuasive. He conveyed a sense of genuine and passionate conviction. Miliukov objected mainly to the second point and argued that in the circumstances it was impossible and, at best, futile, to propose any sort of peace negotiations to our Allies. Tsereteli continued to insist—and his protestations made a somewhat comic impression—that, if only the basic idea, the directive, were recognized, Miliukov would discover those subtle diplomatic procedures by which the directive could be implemented. But Miliukov would not budge at all on this second point. He also dug in his heels as firmly on the matter of annexations and indemnities.

I wonder now whether it would not have been better for Miliukov to have given Kerensky an ultimatum then, not solely because of those ill-fated words, but also because of the idea behind them, an idea which was included in the declaration although admittedly in softer and deliberately ambiguous terms. This matter has importance for me personally, in retrospect. As in the beginning, when Miliukov threatened to resign over the question of Mikhail, so now, too, I felt that his resignation would be disastrous for the international situation and for our Allies' attitude toward us. I thought that, if necessary, we should make even the greatest concessions simply to keep Miliukov in the government. Now I thought that a bit of Machiavellianism might be possible. I recall that Miliukov and I were discussing and correcting the text of the declaration during lunch at the Hotel European, having come directly from the Congress of the Party of the People's Freedom, which had opened on 25 March in the auditorium of the Mikhailovsky Theatre. I was trying to persuade him to agree to include in the declaration an explanation of what Russia did not want from the war, so that "annexations and indemnities" would figure only by inference. I said that these words admitted very broad and subjective interpretation, that, insofar as they included a rejection of aggression, they conformed with out views too, but that they certainly did not have any meaning that could bind one at a future peace conference should the war end in our favour. I remember that we changed the text several times before we eventually found words acceptable to Miliukov. There was still a certain *reservatio mentalis* in his acceptance. But, to take another instance, compare President Wilson's successive declarations, for example, the one which maintained that the present war must end without any victors, with those which dramatized and accompanied America's declaration of war; do they not contain blatant contradictions? Of course, it is impossible to suppose that a simple governmental declaration which has no contractual nature is binding on all subsequent governments. But even the government which has issued the declaration is bound by it only insofar as it contains certain indisputable principles of government policy. It was long ago established that the "principle" of "without annexations and indemnities" could not be accepted, that the statement is ambiguous and in practice it provides no solution. It is not without reason that subsequently the term "disannexation" was invented. It would naturally be difficult to reconcile the transformation of the Dardanelles and Bosphorus into a Russian canal with a strict interpretation of the declaration. But if the circumstances ever made this transformation possible, who would remember the treaty and who would ever choose to use it as an argument against Russia? It would be a different matter if the Russian government, *expressis verbis*, renounced potential gains which had been guaranteed by international treaties and informed the other contracting parties of this renunciation. But this was not, and indeed could not be, done by Miliukov. He himself at a Party congress after he had resigned quite sincerely and convincingly maintained and argued that he had not conceded anything substantial and had not damaged Russia's interests in any respect. But on the other hand, it is hard to deny that this position was artificial. This artificiality, though, was not a matter of the interpretation of the declaration, but lay in the gulf that in fact divided Miliukov's attitude to the war and its problems from the attitude of the Socialist groups which were influencing Kerensky. I recall an occasion when this awkwardness was somehow particularly marked and painfully felt. It happened a few days after the Provisional Government had received a delegation of French and British Socialists. Miliukov made a speech which was wholly consistent and characteristic in tone, and which essentially conformed to Russia's traditional foreign policy in war-time. Kerensky spoke after Miliukov. He spoke Russian which Miliukov translated into English (and one of the Frenchmen translated from English to French). This is where a striking contradiction was really felt, a contradiction in spirit, in the premise itself. Now it became clear that within the Provisional Government there were two fundamental trends that were mutually hostile. There was no doubt that sooner or later— rather sooner than later—the unnatural Kerensky-Miliukov alliance would collapse. It is here that I find an answer to the question I raised above, whether it would not have been better if Miliukov had given an ultimatum before the 28 March declaration and resigned from the Provisional Government without waiting for the mutiny of troops of 20-23 April, which was incited by a statement from the Foreign Minister on 18 April. I think that Miliukov entered the government for the right reasons, and for those same reasons he should have stayed in it, fighting to the end in the interests of his cause. From the very start the revolution created compromises, unnatural combinations. Just as the Provisional Government's treatment of the Soviet of Workers' and Soldiers' Deputies was a compromise, so, too, was the Cabinet's accommodation of two men who were absolutely incapable of seeing eye to eye, Kerensky and Miliukov. These compromises proved to be unsound and did not halt the catastrophic course of the Russian revolution. But in the circumstances they were inevitable, and for us Kadets to have refused them would have meant taking the view that "the worse it gets, the better", or, at the least, it would have meant washing our hands of everything. We then would have even more bitterly felt our responsibility for later events.

Although up to this point a great deal has been said about Miliukov's role in the Provisional Government, I have only dealt with the aspect of his foreign policy. I must say that in my mind, at least, this remains the most brilliant aspect. I do not remember that Miliukov ever raised questions of domestic policy or demanded that any resolute measures be taken. More than he should have, he relied both on the national instinct of the Russian people and on their sensible realization of their own interest. He did not understand, would not understand, and could not accept the fact that the Russian people were opposed to the three-year war, that they were fighting it unwillingly, under the lash, without appreciating its significance or aims, that they were exhausted by it and that the revolution was received with sympathy because they hoped that it would lead to an early peace. He did not know that the noxious seeds, which irresponsible troublemakers had early started to sow in the army, would fall on such receptive ground there. For that reason he did not make a determined, last-ditch stand against permitting the passengers of the famous sealed railway-coach to cross the borders of Russia. One must say that in the matter of these passengers the Provisional Government harboured great illusions. It was thought that because Lenin and Co. were being "imported" by the Germans, they would be completely discredited in the eyes of the public and their propagandizing would have no success. Indeed, at political meetings the subject of "the sealed coach" was always very successful. But that did not prevent the growth of the most furious and destructive propaganda in *Pravda, Okopnaya Pravda*, and a number of other anarchical papers. Now, of course, the Bolsheviks are showing us how a shameless government can, without reservation, stifle a hostile press. The Provisional Government was bound by its own declarations about free speech, by its whole ideology. Its attitude toward newspaper propaganda was completely passive. This passive attitude also in part revealed the government's awareness of its own impotence, which prevented it from taking retribution for such explicitly criminal actions as the seizure of Kshesinskaya's mansion and the conversion of it into a stronghold and pulpit of unbridled Bolshevism. Now of course, it is easy to blame the Provisional Government for this passivity. But if one thinks back to that period and again remembers the prevailing mood, then it is clear that the government could not have acted otherwise without the risk of isolating itself. Who would have supported it? The St. Petersburg garrison was not under governmental control. The "bourgeois" classes, unorganized and non-militant, would have been on its side, of course, but would not have gone beyond Platonic sympathy. But for this crisis such sympathy was not enough, although it came from many sections of the population.

I had occasion not long ago to discuss these matters with Miliukov. We discussed the question of whether there would have been a chance of preventing the catastrophe if at the outset the Provisional Government had boldly asserted its authority, used the support of the State Duma, not allowed the Soviet and Executive Committee any political role, and arrested the ringleaders if there had been any resistance. I regarded, and still do regard, this possibility as a purely theoretical one. But Miliukov maintained that in the early days of the revolution the State Duma controlled the garrison and, if this opportunity had not been missed, the situation could have been saved. Obviously, the matter of Mikhail is important here. If the dynasty had remained on the throne, the government and its prestige would have been preserved. But I do not see how the Provisional Government could have survived without a monarch. What would have preserved its prestige and authority? Or, more importantly, how would it have coped with the war, that touchstone of the whole revolution?

I well remember that Miliukov more than once raised the matter of the need for a tougher and more determined fight against the growing anarchy. Others did so, too. But I do not remember any definite practical measures ever proposed or debated by the Provisional Government. It was paralyzed by the lack of both a well-organized police force and an unquestionably loyal military force. Here, too, were the seeds of ruin, and its spread could not be curtailed by all the Provisional Government's tremendous energy in basic legislation. Moreover, every one of the Ministers was so hard pressed in his own department that no one had time to give any practical thought to the problems of other departments and to suggest any concrete measures. In private conferences only general political issues were discussed. Of course, Miliukov more than once considered, for example, whether to put an end to the disgusting scandal that was going on unhampered both outside and inside Kshesinskaya's house. But how was this to be done? To this question we had no answer.

The story of Miliukov's resignation undoubtedly has been very fully told in the already-completed first volume of his *History of the Russian Revolution*. His resignation was in fact, of course, the work of the Socialists, aided on this occasion by Albert Thomas, who had arrived in St. Petersburg on 9 April. I do not remember whether it was before Thomas's arrival or in the second or third week in April that Miliukov told me during one of my morning visits that he was really considering whether it would not be better for him to surrender the Foreign Ministry portfolio to Tereshchenko ("At least he is not completely ignorant in these matters and will be able at any rate to talk to Ambassadors") so that Manuilov could take over the Ministry of Finance (or Shingarev, perhaps; and Manuilov, the Ministry of Agriculture) and hand the Education portfolio over to himself, Miliukov. But I did not support this idea and Miliukov himself soon dropped it. It was just at this time that Chernov returned to Russia and the campaign against Miliukov began in earnest. At the Provisional Government's joint session with the Committee of the State Duma and the Executive Committee of the Soviet of Deputies, at which matters of foreign policy were discussed and Chernov declared that it was time for Russia to stop talking to Europe like "a poor relation", he said openly, with his typically vulgar mannerisms, sugary smile, and grimaces, that both he and his friends had infinite respect for P. N. Miliukov and considered his participation in the Provisional Government essential, but in their opinion he could better deploy his talents in another post, even if only as Minister of Education. At the same time a nasty incident involving Kerensky occurred, in connection with a semi-official communiqué which he passed to the Press Bureau announcing that a government statement on matters of foreign policy was about to be published. That this communiqué had come from Kerensky I learned from L. L'vov (the head of the Bureau). I knew perfectly well that the Provisional Government had mentioned nothing of the sort, and I saw Kerensky's action as an underhanded trick, if not a provocation. I immediately informed Miliukov at the Provisional Government's sitting that was in session at the time. At the end of the sitting Miliukov asked who had given the press a deliberately untruthful communiqué. Kerensky was somewhat disconcerted and tried to shirk the issue by saying that he was not responsible for the way the press reported his words, but in the end he declared that as things were he considered a statement necessary. Then Miliukov told Prince L'vov that, if Kerensky did not refute the communiqué, he, Miliukov, would hand in his resignation immediately. Since it was already late afternoon and everybody was tired, it was decided to debate the matter in the evening. There was a very stormy session at which Kerensky felt himself quite isolated, since even his strongest supporters found his method disgraceful and intolerable. He was forced to concede and telephoned (from my office) the required denial. At the same time, however, it was suggested that our declaration on the problems of the war had not been officially communicated to our Allies and would, therefore, seem to be a document for internal consumption only which would, of course, undermine its importance. It was, therefore, requested that diplomatic representatives be officially informed of the view of the Provisional Government on this matter. It was difficult to argue against this, and Miliukov had to agree; next the decision was taken to debate the Foreign Ministers' note at a full session of the Provisional Government, and this was done. At the time, A. I. Guchkov was ill with a weak heart, and so the session took place at his house. I remember very clearly that the first reading of Miliukov's draft impressed everybody, even Kerensky, as eminently acceptable, and, moreover, as indicative of Miliukov's great compliance and willingness to meet the demands of his opponents. For this reason there was hardly any debate initially, but when Kerensky started to carp at isolated words, suggesting most unsuitable variants, the atmosphere began to deteriorate, and the usual personal antagonism made itself felt in loud voices and sharp words. Nevertheless, they finally managed to resolve differences and agree on a text, the one that was published. At the end of the session, I remember, Miliukov stressed that the government was, therefore, in complete agreement on the document and was accepting responsibility for its contents. Kerensky made no objections. Evidently, on this occasion his common sense and a wise handling of the matter proved stronger than party blinkers. On the other hand, Kerensky apparently did not find it necessary to consult his friends, being honestly convinced that for them, too, the statement would be quite acceptable. It was published on 20 April. Then events occurred which we all know and which were at the time reported in detail in the press. Since the demonstrations were directed against Miliukov, the Provisional Government was forced to announce officially that the note had been approved without dissension from any quarter. In point of fact, the whole demonstration was a bare-faced bluff and sparked off impressive counter-demonstrations. But the general mood became strained and tense. The fact that in this matter Kerensky had been forced to join forces formally with Miliukov probably exacerbated his personal antagonism. The Socialists doggedly went on with their work; Thomas played an ambiguous role and made slighting and hostile references to Miliukov.* But since, by

---

*At this same time the Provisional Government decided it was necessary to reinforce its ranks with Socialists (see the declaration of 23 April). Miliukov was against this in principle and agreed to the text of the declaration very much against his will. I am going to talk about this again separately.

that time, Miliukov had decided once and for all not to yield, it was obvious that a crisis had to arise on the initiative of the Provisional Government. It did. What part the other Kadet Ministers played in it I am not prepared to say. Miliukov was offered the education portfolio, he turned it down categorically, and he left the session no longer a Minister. The next morning Vinaver and I visited him at the request of the Central Committee and for a long time tried hard to persuade him to stay and accept the education portfolio. We felt that Miliukov's resignation coming at the same time as the introduction of the Socialists into the government would be the beginning of the end. Of course, we also thought that Miliukov, if he stayed in the government even as Minister of Education, would have a chance to influence foreign policy and keep abreast of it. He could do so in a special body formed from members of the Provisional Government whose job, it was envisaged, would be to handle simultaneously matters of defence and of foreign policy. This body had been conceived as a move against Miliukov. We suggested to him that in the changed circumstances he use the body in the interests of his cause and could set his membership in this body as a condition of his continued participation in the government. Miliukov would not agree. He argued at first, but, when all the arguments had been exhausted, he said exactly this: "Your arguments may be correct, but I have an inner voice which tells me that I must not comply with them. Whenever I have a clear and definite feeling, even though it is unsupported by reason, that a given line of conduct is needed, I obey it. I cannot do otherwise." We realized there was nothing more to be said and withdrew. That moment marked the beginning of the real rift between Miliukov and the Provisional Government.

I have already referred to the declaration and appeal of 23 April in which there was a promise to invite the Socialists to join the government. This appeal was a development of the notion (strongly urged almost from the very outset by Guchkov, and later, Manuilov) that the Provisional Government should resign after telling the country what it had done and why it considered any further efforts useless; a sort of epitaph or political testament. But in the event the appeal did not proclaim the government's resignation. What it did do was give a complete picture of what was happening in the country and state the alternatives: either the ruin and loss of the "revolution's gains", or the people's voluntary support for the authority of the government. Kokoshkin was given the job of drafting the document. Miliukov later maintained that, thanks to Kerensky, Kokoshkin's text became an abstract sociological discourse devoid of any practical value. This is an exaggeration, Kerensky—and not he himself, but the editorial board of *Delo Naroda*—introduced into the appeal only a few lines which in a rather vague and abstract way explained the existing disorder by the fact that the old social and political ties had broken down before new bonds had time to form and strengthen. Of course, this was "sociology", but it was completely harmless, and it was not this that gave the appeal its predominant character. If it was a feeble document (and I find it very feeble), it was not Kerensky's fault and even less, of course, Kokoshkin's. It was weak in its underlying tone, and it cannot be denied that its ideology, which regarded it as supremely important that citizens voluntarily accept the authority of the government they themselves had elected, was much akin to the ideology of anarchism. In any case, the crux of the matter lay not in these admonitions but in the appeal to the Socialists. Apparently, the Provisional Government itself did not believe that they would respond. But the Socialists realized that another rejection could be used as a powerful weapon against them and would put them in a position of "irresponsible critics" and "watchdogs", an extremely difficult role. They entered the Cabinet. One could say, in point of fact, that from that moment the days of the Provisional Government, which had been put in power by the "victorious revolution", were numbered, that we had entered a period of ministerial crises, each of which weakened the government, and that it was not possible to call a halt on the road which led to the Bolshevik triumph. Even if Miliukov had not resigned in early May, he still could not have travelled the same road as Tsereteli and Skobelev.

The Liaison Commission, which I have already mentioned more than once, was formed by the Soviet of Workers' and Soldiers' Deputies on 10 March, and its first members were Chkheidze, Skobelev, Steklov-Nakhamkes, Filippovsky, and Sukhanov. At the end of March Tsereteli replaced Steklov. If my memory is correct, however, they at first served jointly. Chernov appeared much later. During the first weeks of the Provisional Government the Liaison Commission met often, about three times a week and sometimes more, always late in the evening after the Provisional Government session, which in these instances was always abbreviated. The leading figure at these meetings was Steklov. I first met him then, and I did not suspect that he was a Jew or that his euphonic pseudonym covered up his far from euphonic real name. Even less, of course, was it known—it was later revealed to me by L. L'vov—that Nakhamkes had made the most humble and servile applications to "legalize" his pseudonym and officially substitute it for his real name. His name organically combined the words "impudent lout" (*nakhal*) and "boor" (*kham*), and perfectly suited his manner, which I found repulsive from the very first. His tone was that of a man who believed that the Provisional Government existed only by his grace and only for as long as it pleased him. He acted like a tutor seeing to it that his charge behaved properly, did not indulge in mischief, carried out his orders, and always remembered what he was allowed and what he was forbidden to do; with this went an awareness of his own power, which kept coming to the surface, and an emphasizing of his magnanimity. How many times I had to listen to words which directly or indirectly meant: "You (that is, the Provisional Government) perfectly well know, after all, that if we so desired we could take over the government without hindrance, and ours would be the strongest and most authoritative government. If we have not done so and for the moment do not do so, it is merely because we consider for the time being you suit the historical moment. We have agreed to allow you to rule, but for that very reason you must remember your place with respect to us and must not forget yourselves or adopt any serious and important measures without consulting us and getting our approval. You must remember that, if we so wish, you will be gone this very instant, since you have no independent meaning and importance." He never let slip an opportunity to expound these ideas. I remember that on one occasion Prince L'vov mentioned the stream of greetings and good wishes arriving daily from all parts of Russia, hundreds of telegrams promising the Provisional Government help and support. "We", retorted Steklov immediately, "could show you right now far more, tenfold more, telegram endorsed by hundreds and thousands of organized citizens, which ask us to take over the government." Another proclamation was this: "We",—that is, the Executive Committee—"are shielding you with our bodies from hostile attacks; we are instilling the masses, who accept our authority with trust in you." This line was particularly annoying to Kerensky who, as "democracy's hostage" and still formally a Deputy Chairman of the Executive Committee, thought, or wanted others to think, that he was winning the hearts of the "broad masses" for the Provisional Government. For that reason he could stand Nakhamkes less than anybody and reacted with great irritation to his tone. He also thought that his position in the Provisional Government did not allow him to argue with Steklov and deflate him. He would, therefore, often avoid attending sessions with the Liaison Commission and, whenever he did, it was only as an "observer", sitting as far away as possible, maintaining a stubborn silence and glancing only angrily and contemptuously with his ever squinting, short-sighted eyes at the speaker or the others. But when the session was over and he was alone with his ministerial colleagues, he would often heatedly attack Prince L'vov, accusing him of being too lax and considerate, and expressing surprise that L'vov let some statement or other of Nakhamkes pass without a proper answer.

It should be said that on occasion Steklov aroused the annoyance of even his own "friends", or rather, of the other members of the Liaison Commission, since he apparently had few friends. At times Chkheidze or Skobelev would interrupt a statement of his, or immediately after it, would observe that Steklov was speaking only for himself on the matter in hand or that he was expressing his personal opinion and "we had not decided this". This, however, did not worry Steklov in the slightest . . . It even happened that he would then and there try to argue with his colleagues. But I do not know if any of them was capable of matching Steklov's unlimited self-assurance and his brash identification of his own voice with that of the "toiling masses". Later, when the story of his servile application ("self-prostration") became known, it was used against him, and he was forced for a time, for a long time even, to keep in the background. But during the first two weeks he really did have some importance. At the First Congress of delegates of the Soviet of Workers' and Soldiers' Deputies on 29 March, he recounted the history of the relationship between the Provisional Government and the Executive Committee, and he expounded a scheme for introducing Soviet commissars into all departments "to keep under vigilant surveillance all the activities of the Provisional Government". This idea of commissars gave rise to one of the most bitter controversies. It was only dropped when the entry of Socialists onto the Provisional Government made the latter seem more "reliable" to the Soviet of Workers' and Soldiers' Deputies.

Of the other members of the Liaison Commission, two Filippovsky and Sukhanov, hardly ever spoke, at least not while I was working for the Provisional Government. Next to Steklov, Skobelev was the most frequent speaker. I had not known him before either. He was one of the most insignificant of those talentless and limited men who accidently became famous throughout Russia as a *porte-voix* of the "working masses", because the Provisional Government provided a national podium for their political speeches, which were inspired and sometimes directly dictated from behind the scenes. He tried hard, in good faith, to be a *porte-voix*, but he was by no means a great speaker. For all I know, in a political meeting sympathetic to him he may have made an impression, but here, where there were no stereotypes and where only the substance of a speech was important, he was invariably deficient, feebly, boring, and timid in the extreme. Nevertheless, it cannot be denied that he was more attractive than those close to him. He seemed ingenuous, more sincere, more honest than they. Perhaps he was affected by the atmosphere of the State Duma and realized more fully the enormity of the difficulties that had arisen.

Chkheidze is a much more colourful figure than Skobelev. I learned from Shul'gin not long ago in Kiev, that in the very first days, if not hours, of the revolution, Chkheidze completely gave way to despair, clasped his head in his hands, and declared that all was lost. There was always, in my eyes, something tragi-comic about him, in his overall appearance, his facial expression, his way of speaking, his accent. Of course, the real tragedy was that a man like Chkheidze should become a "leader of democracy" for all of Russia, a chairman of the Soviet of Workers' Deputies, an influential figure, and, at least at that time, a prospective candidate for the chairmanship of the Constituent Assembly and perhaps for the presidency of the Russian Republic. At meetings with the Liaison Commission he spoke whenever a statement or an enquiry needed additional emphasis. It is worth noting that even he appears to have thought unfavourably of Steklov.

Joint sessions with the Liaison Commission did not take place every day, nor did they have fixed days. The request for a meeting usually came from the Commission itself: the message (Chkheidze usually sent it) would state that the Commission would like to meet with the Provisional Government to discuss a few matters. However, in most instances the government was not informed beforehand what points would be raised, and so there were sometimes quite amusing surprises, revealing the extent to which views on the relative importance of some fact or measure differed. I remember that one matter which received much attention in the early days was the funeral of victims of the revolution. The Soviet of Workers' Deputies, with considerable effrontery, wanted to monopolize this ceremony. Without advising the Provisional Government, the Executive Committee fixed the day, published the order of ceremony, and chose the place for the fraternal grave, the Palace Square, where, as is known, they proceeded even to dig the grave. After long, exhausting, and absurd squabbling, this matter was finally settled, the government came to an agreement with the Executive Committee, and there followed a grandiose demonstration of the type whose success depends partly on hordes of idlers who are ready to join in or watch solemn processions, and partly on that mood which craves to make some sort of demonstration and finds satisfaction in it.

As I have already said, at the end of March Tsereteli appeared at the sessions of the Liaison Commission. As far as I was concerned he was an unknown quantity. At the time of the Second Duma I had heard him speak from the platform more than once, but I had not had an opportunity to meet him. The first impression he made was undoubtedly agreeable. His name was surrounded with an aura of genuine and tragic political martyrdom.

His brief career in the second Duma, which won him everyone's sympathy, ended with a ten-year term of exile which was spent, at least in the beginning, in very distressing conditions. His appearance was somehow appropriate to one's picture of his moral character. His oriental face is handsome and refined, and his big, dark eyes now flash, now film over in wistful reverie. He is certainly an outstanding speaker. His accent is less marked, less coarse than Chkheidze's, and it adds a particularly expressive force to what he is saying. He is capable of achieving great dynamism, especially in a sympathetic atmosphere and when he is dealing with subjects dear to Social-Democrats. But at the same time he can be, and not infrequently is, intolerably bombastic, essentially vapid, and false. In this respect two of his speeches especially stick in my mind, one, delivered at the solemn session of all four Dumas on 27 April, the other, at the Moscow State Conference. It was particularly painful to hear the latter speech, so obvious was it that Tsereteli himself did not believe what he was saying. However, his words usually conveyed a sense of great conviction and sincerity, and this is one of the factors in his success. Of course, if one looks to his speeches for profundity of content, a wealth of ideas, and catholic learning, then one will be sorely disappointed. The scope of Tsereteli's ideas is very narrow and consists, in fact, of very ordinary Marxist platitudes absorbed in student days. Anything beyond these platitudes, anything that requires deep insight, individuality, or independent thought, leaves Tsereteli floundering.

I had occasion to meet him more personally in mid-September 1917, at the conferences with representatives of the political parties that Kerensky organized, as a result of which the last Cabinet (with Kishkin, Konovalov, Tret'yakov, Smirnov, Malyantovich, and Maslov) was formed and the Council of the Russian Republic instituted. The most distinctive feature of his outlook then was fear of the growing might of Bolshevism. I remember our private conversation about the possibility of the Bolsheviks seizing power. "Of course", he said, "they won't last more than two or three weeks, but just think what destruction there will be! We must avoid this at all cost." There was a note of genuine panic in his voice. At the time he believed in the redeeming power of the

Council of the Russian Republic. He (or those who shared his views) had invented this title. He suggested it to me on the evening I arrived as arranged at Skobelev's apartment to discuss the draft of the ministerial declaration which Tsereteli had drawn up. That evening I had an important appointment elsewhere, and I wanted to leave a bit earlier. I confess that because of this I probably paid insufficient attention both to the text of the declaration and to the suggestion to name the newly formed body the "Council of the Russian Republic". I must add, however, in my own defence, that previous experience had made me sceptical toward declarations of any sort. I was gradually coming to the conclusion that this endless bargaining over isolated words and phrases, this die-hard stubbornness in defending some and disputing others, was pitiful and futile sophistry, of importance and interest only to party circles, various central committees and so on, but without relevance to and totally divorced from everyday life. The contents of the declaration had been elucidated beforehand at the conference in the Winter Palace, where the Ministry's programme had been elaborated. The editing of this programme had seemed to me of minor importance. Because of this, there were in the original draft which Tsereteli wrote and I accepted two or three unfortunate passages which were corrected or removed by A. Ya. Galpern, who was then Head of the Secretariat of the Provisional Government; (I cannot now remember what these *lapsus* were). Tsereteli protested on the phone but eventually conceded. As far as the name "Council of the Russian Republic" is concerned, it was, of course, up to me, as a Kadet, to make strong protest, since we Kadets considered it quite wrong to fix a formal name to a temporary regime which had been established in time of revolution and was to last only until the Constituent Assembly. I remember when Tsereteli said to me with a certain exaltation: "We've coined the title 'Council of the Russian Republic'. It's good, isn't it? Don't you think so, Vladimir Dmitrievich? I think it will make a great impression and win immediate favour." I replied that a more suitable title would have been "Council of the Russian State" or "Provisional Government Council"* even though the first title made

---

*It is remarkable that this latter title was later stoutly defended by A. A. Dem'yanov at the session of the Provisional Govt. at which the draft was read and passed.

the new body sound too much like the former State Council and the latter put it on a par, as it were, with an ordinary government consultative board. In any event, I did not oppose Tsereteli's suggestion. . .

I shall have to return to the matter of the "Council of the Russian Republic", which I have touched upon here only in connexion with Tsereteli. As is known, he left for the Caucasus just at that time, the end of September, and did not come back to St. Petersburg until the beginning of November, after the Bolshevik seizure of power. Then, when he met me in the Town Duma, he said: "Yes, of course, what we were doing then was a futile attempt to hold back a destructive, elemental torrent with flimsy slivers of wood."

At this point I wish to include just one more episode that has nothing to do with Tsereteli. But it does have a place in the story of the creation of the Council of the Russian Republic. When the text of the statute relating to it had been settled, I arranged with P. N. Malyantovich, the newly appointed Minister of Justice, to visit him and to do the final editing. He suggested a very late hour, 12 o'clock, and I agreed. I found him in the study I remembered so well from my childhood at the apartment of the Procurator-General. . . He was extremely worried and told me the cause of his concern. The notorious N. D. Sokolov, who two or three months previously had been appointed Senator of the First Department by Kerensky, had had a clash with the chairman on the question of uniforms. He refused to abide by the Senators' decision to keep uniforms at open sessions and general meetings. He had appeared at one session in a frock-coat, apparently had a violent argument with Vrasky (I wasn't at this meeting), and had had to leave. Then he had sent a written statement to the Minister of Justice, pointing out that the Senate had acted illegally and arbitrarily in requiring senators to put on "the emblems of slavery" (these are the words he used to denote the buttons on the uniform with their image of the two-headed eagle above the law) and also demanding that the matter be settled by legislation in the spirit of democracy. Malyantovich was in a terrible quandary. "What do you think should be done?" he asked me. I answered ironically that I had not given this grave and complicated matter a great deal of thought, and I added that, if I were he, I would throw N. D. Sokolov's statement into the waste-paper basket under the table. "How can you say that! After all, you know Nikolai Dmitrievich. He won't let the matter rest. I'm thinking of appointing some sort of commission to handle it. The main problem is that it is very difficult at the moment to introduce new buttons. Where would we get them from? And they would constitute another big expense for the senators . . ." Since I didn't answer, he concluded with a sigh: "Perhaps you will think of something a little later . . ."

It was with such trivial, pathetic nonsense that a member of the Provisional Government was concerned a month before its overthrow . . . The question of the buttons apparently remained open to the very end . . .

NOW, AFTER MORE THAN A YEAR, when I wish to relive in my mind the first two months of the Provisional Government's existence, my memory conjures up a rather chaotic picture. I recall separate episodes, heated quarrels which sometimes arose quite unexpectedly, endless debates which at times caused a session to drag on until late at night. I remember the feverish activity which began every morning and was interrupted only by lunch and dinner. I was living at my home on Morskaya, five minutes' walk from the Mariinsky Palace, and this was very convenient. I remember the endless stream of telephone calls and the daily visitors, which made concentration impossible. I remember an atmosphere in which everything that happened seemed unreal. It was hard to believe that we could successfully fulfil our two main tasks: to pursue the war and to steer the country safely to a Constituent Assembly . . .

We know that the Provisional Government's resolution to summon a special conference in order to draw up the laws governing elections to the Constituent Assembly was passed only at the end of March. This body was to be constituted in a way (nominations put forward by groups and parties) which would ensure full confidence in it. But unfortunately it took a very long time. The Executive Committee of the Soviet of Workers' Deputies, which was terribly late in presenting its candidates, was in fact mostly to blame. It must, however, be said that the concept of the Constituent Assembly was inherently defective, and this was instinctively felt from the beginning. Later I often heard opinions such as the following expressed: the Provisional Government, in the earliest days, should have founded a small commission composed of a few very able and competent lawyers, charged them to draft within a fortnight the laws governing the elections, and then set the earliest possible date for the elections, for example, May. I remember that (somewhat surprisingly) L. M. Bramson, among others, expressed this idea. Since my first days as Head of the Secretariat I myself had persistently and frequently broached with Prince L'vov the need to raise the matter as concretely and as soon as possible and to settle it. But there were always other, more urgent matters to cope with which permitted no delay. When at last this special consultative body was formed and the work of elaborating the law began, the machinery was so complicated and cumbersome that it became impossible to expect that the work would soon be concluded and that elections could be set for a date in the near future. Does it, therefore, follow that the other plan—the setting up of a small commission, the speedy laying down of the laws, and the earliest possible date for elections— was both feasible and expedient? I don't think so. In the first place, I have no doubt that a campaign would have been immediately initiated against the government, accusing it of intending to lay down the laws academically and bureaucratically. The government would have been blamed for any shortcomings in the law. The authority of those framing the laws and, of course, the scheme they executed would have been undermined. I think that even those framing the laws would have been stymied on certain basic problems of principle, such as, for example, the matter of whether the electoral system should be by majority or proportional, or of whether active army and navy personnel could participate in the elections, or of how elections in outlying districts should be organized. But even supposing that these difficulties could have been overcome, how was it possible to organize elections in a Russia racked from top to bottom by revolution, in a Russia which as yet had neither democratic self-government nor a smooth working machinery of local government? And what about elections in the army? But, of course, the greatest risk would have been the actual convening of the Constituent Assembly. Simple-minded people might imagine this assembly and its role to be theoretically as follows: it would meet, work out the basic laws, settle the question of the form of government, appoint the government and invest it with full powers to end the war, and would then dissolve itself . . . One can imagine this, but who believes that it could actually have happened like that? If any government had survived until the Constituent Assembly, its convening would undoubtedly had been the beginning of anarchy.

Now the Constituent Assembly experiment has been carried out. Probably the Bolsheviks themselves did not think in October that this body would be abolished so easily as early as the beginning of January, two months after the revolution. As we know, one of the accusations the Bolsheviks levelled at the Provisional Government was that it had delayed elections . . . But when the Constituent Assembly no longer suited their needs, they disbanded it without the slightest hesitation. If the Provisional Government had felt that it had genuine power, it would have promptly announced that the Constituent Assembly would be convened when the war was over, and, of course, this would in fact have been the only correct solution once Mikhail Aleksandrovich's rejection of the throne made it necessary to raise the question of the form of government. But the Provisional Government did not feel that it had real power. Since the very beginning of its existence, those in society who were sensible and moderate but, alas, timid, unorganized, accustomed only to obey and incapable of commanding, were on one side, and, on the other, was organized rascality with its obtuse, fanatic, and frequently dishonest ringleaders.

The question of the army at once became the centre of gravity of the situation.

About three weeks after the revolution, from 20 March onward, deputations from the battle front began to arrive in St. Petersburg. The purpose of their coming was, on the one hand, to announce to the Provisional Government their readiness to support the new regime and to defend freedom, and on the other, to size up the true relationship between the Provisional Government and the Soviet of Workers' Deputies. Deputations arrived daily, from various fronts and various units, more or less numerous in composition and led by commanders and officers with red badges and red banners. The Provisional Government nearly always received them in the rotunda of the Mariinsky Palace. I remember how surprised I was in the beginning by the scene of the interior of this Palace, and how hard it was to reconcile it with old memories of the era of the pre-reform Council and my service in the State Chancellery. In those days the Mariinsky Palace was the sanctuary of the higher bureaucracy. It housed the State Council with the State Chancellery, the Committee of Ministers and its secretariat, as well as the Office of Petitions addressed to His Imperial Majesty. In the magnificent apartments of the palace, with their velvet carpets, heavy draperies and gilded furniture, extraordinarily stately footmen moved silently about in embroidered liveries and white hose, serving tea and coffee. On Mondays, the day of the Plenum, a sort of agitated solemnity prevailed. There were the imposing figures of generally very aged dignitaries bedecked with ribbons and orders, there were military and court uniforms, subdued conversations, and all this created a sense of inaccessibility, as it were, of separation from vulgar, everyday life. On those days anyone in a lounge suit would have seemed indecently and barbarously inapposite if he had suddenly found himself among those beautifully groomed, elegantly dressed gentlemen of stately comport.

Now all that had vanished completely. The Mariinsky Palace had undergone a radical transformation to "plain living". Hordes of ragged and badly dressed people in jackets and blouses of the most proletarian type invaded its sumptuous salons. The splendid footmen exchanged their liveries for grey, double-breasted jackets and lost all their impressiveness. The solemn and decorous ceremonial of yesterday was replaced by a clamorous scramble. All this may have happened gradually, but it seemed to take a very short time. In the first weeks only the Provisional Government and the Juridical Conference met in the Mariinsky Palace. The "revolutionary" mayor, Iu. N. Glebov, made persistent attempts to get the great hall of the State Duma with its antechamber put at the disposal of the Town Duma for its sessions. I made equally persistent attempts to counter his plan, which fell through. But, nevertheless, the palace very quickly became the headquarters of all sorts of commissions, and, when the conference began its work on electoral law for the Constituent Assembly, there were days when every room including the rotunda was occupied by a commission. During March things had not come to this pass, and the rotunda was nearly always available and was used to receive military deputations.

How painful and distressing it is now to recall those deputations! How often we listened to declarations of readiness to support the "People's Provisional Government" with all power and vigour, to join together to defend the freedom and inviolability of our native land, to ignore troublemakers and foil the schemes of our enemies! What passionate and often rapturous speeches! Admittedly, the soldiers' faces expressed at best a bemused stupidity; admittedly, the officers' words conveyed no sense of self-assurance or authority, and their revolutionary phrases often grated, giving an ominous air to the proceedings. Admittedly, this sudden revolutionary awareness seemed unintelligible and improbable, and silently one asked oneself: Is this not simply the voice of mutiny, is this not a manifestation of an instinctive bridling against all discipline, all obedience? The main subject of the speeches was almost invariably the relations between the Provisional Government and the Soviet of Workers' Deputies. It was often said that the army was confused and disoriented by what seemed to be dual government, that it needed one single government. In answer, government representatives made rather unctuous statements to the effect that there was no duality of power, that there was complete unity, mutual trust, and that there were the best of relations between the Provisional Government and the Soviet of Workers' Deputies. The war also was mentioned, but here a sense of confidence could be felt least of all.

The first deputations made a great impression on both the Provisional Government and the delegates themselves. It seemed as though a spiritual link with the army was being forged and that it would be possible to retain or even re-create a strong and stable military force. But it only seemed so. The deputations from the front made contact not only with the government but also with the

Soviet of Workers' Deputies. The government confined itself to receiving them in the halls of the Mariinsky Palace, listening to them and answering; the deputations shouted "hurrah", and then they went off to the Tavrichesky Palace where a belief in the greatness and omnipotence of the Soviet of Workers' Deputies and its Executive Committee was instilled into them, and all sorts of irresponsible people dealt in demagogic and anarchical propaganda. They found this same propaganda everywhere, at street meetings and in barracks, they came into contact with the extremist and corrupt elements of the St. Petersburg garrison who prided themselves on the fact that "we made the revolution", and they were themselves corrupted. Consequently, the pilgrimages of army deputations to St. Petersburg infected and demoralized the troops, rather than ensuring their good health.

When General Alekseev came to St. Petersburg in the middle of April and gave a summary of feelings in the army, I well remember the horror and despair that swept over me. The conclusion was quite obvious. Notwithstanding all reservations, even then one had to accept that the revolution had struck our armed forces a terrible blow, that demoralization was proceeding rapidly, and that the commanders were powerless. Two different tendencies, two types of men came to light among these commanders. Some very quickly realized that they could hold onto their jobs only by indulging the propagandized soldiers and currying favour with them, by carrying to extremes the new "comradely" relationships, or, to put it bluntly, kowtowing to the troops. These men, of course, only contributed to the collapse of discipline and the loss of a sense of military duty, to the overall destruction of the army. Others would not accept the new order and the new spirit and tried to combat it and show authority, and they became involved in tragic incidents, or proved a nuisance to the higher command and were removed from their posts. In this way the best, strongest, and most conscientious elements gradually disappeared and only pathetic riff-raff or particularly smart fellows who knew how to walk a tightrope between the two extremes remained.

Among my papers are still a few letters I received at the time or later from General N. N. Ignat'ev, a man who had spent his whole life in the army and had commanded the Preobrazhensky Regiment in wartime, a true officer who was also an intelligent, thoughtful, and earnest man. If I am not mistaken, the revolution came when he was either Chief of Staff of the Guard Corps or Commander of the Guards Infantry Division. These letters of his made a strong impression on me. They confirmed my worst suspicions. I don't have them at hand at this moment and so cannot check the dates, but I remember that very soon the following note was heard in the letters: we must get it clearly into our heads that the war is over, that we cannot and must not go on fighting because at heart the army does not want to fight. Intelligent people must find a painless way to end the war, otherwise there will be a catastrophe . . . I showed one of these letters to Guchkov. He read it and handed it back to me, saying that he was receiving stacks of similar letters. "What do you think about it?" I asked. He only shrugged his shoulders and said something to the effect that we must hope for a miracle. But the miracle did not happen, the process continued on its natural and inevitable way and led to the natural and inevitable conclusion.

The Bolshevik Revolution
(October 1917)

In March During a Break in one of the Provisional Government's sessions at which there was conversation about the steady spread of Bolshevik propaganda, Kerensky said, hysterically guffawing as usual: "Just wait, Lenin himself is coming . . . That's when things will really get moving!" This provoked a brief exchange of views among the Ministers. It was already known that Lenin and his friends were intending to avail themselves of the Germans' services in order to get from Switzerland to Russia. It was also known that Germany, apparently on the basis of a careful calculation of the consequences, was prepared to co-operate. If I am not mistaken, Miliukov (yes, he was the one!) asked: "Gentlemen, are we really going to allow them in under the circumstances?" But he got a fairly unanimous reply to the effect that there were no formal grounds for refusing Lenin entry; on the contrary, Lenin had a right to return inasmuch as he had been granted amnesty, and inasmuch as the means to which he was resorting in order to make the journey were not legally criminal ones in law. It was added that, from the point of view of political expediency, Lenin's use of Germany's services would so destroy his prestige that there was no need to fear him. On the whole, they all took a fairly casual view of the dangers arising from the return of the Bolshevik leader. This set the general tone. Bound by its own proclamations about freedom and preoccupied with its constant meetings, the Provisional Government could not manage to counteract even the most extreme and destructive propaganda that was being spread by word of mouth and in the press.

Lenin's arrival and his first speech had a strange and unexpected effect which found expression in the newspapers at the time. Even Steklov-Nakhamkes thought it necessary to say that Lenin had evidently lost touch with the true state of affairs in Russia. *Pravda* also took a while to rise to the level of its ideological master. The Executive Committee's initial embarrassment quickly changed to open hostility. But Lenin's colossal perseverance and self-confidence could not, of course, be held in check so easily. Everything that followed showed how even the last detail had been clear-sightedly planned. The plan was put into operation immediately, step by step; its key factors were the army's exhaustion and the demoralization that had started rapidly and, one might say, catastrophically at the front as a result of the St. Petersburg revolt.

From my recollections I must say that the Provisional Government was surprisingly inactive in the face of this destructivity. Lenin was hardly ever mentioned. I recall Kerensky saying as early as April, some time after Lenin's arrival, that he wanted to visit him and talk with him, and in answer to puzzled questions he explained: "After all, he is living in complete isolation, knows nothing, sees everything through the spectacles of his imagination; he has nobody to give him the slightest help in understanding what is going on." As far as I know, the visit did not take place. I do not know whether Lenin turned it down or whether Kerensky himself gave up his idea. Then, as I think I have already noted, the Provisional Government repeatedly discussed the disgraceful business of Kshesinskaya's house, a private property blatantly seized by force and daily subjected to damage and destruction. But the matter never got beyond talk. When Kshesinskaya's lawyer brought a suit before the magistrate, in order to have the organization which had arbitrarily taken possession of the building ejected, Kerensky pointed out with pleasure that they had taken the right steps at last. But when he was asked how the magistrate's verdict would be executed, he replied that that was not his business but the business of the administration, the executive body, the Ministry of Internal Affairs—that Ministry being at the time non-existent. As is known, they managed to evict the Bolsheviks in the end, but the damage was done; they had made full and thorough use of their street platform.

In the initial and partly organized demonstration against the Provisional Government, from 19 to 21 April, when soldiers came to the Mariinsky Palace with placards demanding Miliukov's resignation, the Bolsheviks' role was still unclear. This demonstration was put down without any trouble, as is known. The vast majority of St. Petersburg citizens came out quite clearly on the side of the Provisional Government. At that time Guchkov was ill, and the meetings took place at his home. I remember that troubled day, which began as the troops came to the square in front of the Mariinsky Palace and ended with enthusiastic ovations for Miliukov and Guchkov at a protracted meeting outside the Ministry of War. On that day the great moral strength of the Provisional Government could still be felt, but, alas!, it remained unexploited . . . It was then that, as though for the first time, St. Petersburg sensed the possibility of further upheavals and said with a majority voice that it did not want them.

The story of the July days, when the troops demonstrated for the second time, and it seemed like a genuine attempt at rebellion, will one day be analysed in detail and the whole secret course of events laid bare. I simply wish to recall my own personal experiences and impressions. I had long ago ceased to be Head of the Secretariat of the Provisional Government. My official activities were, however, fairly varied, since I was working in the Juridical Conference and in the Commissions and Plenum of the Conference to draw up the laws for the Constituent Assembly elections. In addition, I was a member of a commission to review and implement the Criminal Code. How sad it is, by the way, to recall now that intensive activity which absorbed so much work, energy, and time, work that was often of the very highest calibre (I mean, of course, the work of the whole body, not my own personal effort), and which has remained absolutely fruitless and half-forgotten.

For some time there had been rumours that the Bolsheviks were preparing an armed uprising. Kerensky was at the front. Propaganda in the streets, at public meetings, and in the newspapers was growing daily more and more unrestrained. After the first news of success during the first days of the uprising (18 June), alarming rumours began to spread. An atmosphere of anxiety and depression was developing.

We had had a meeting for 2 July on the premises of the Central Committee, at 8.30 P.M. as usual. On my way there after dinner I noticed considerable excitement as I approached the Quay. There were many soldiers along the Millionnaya, and some units were standing on the Field of Mars, near the beginning of the Millionnaya. There were loud conversations, with talk of demonstrations coming from the other side of the Neva. Suvorov Square was blocked by people. Already as I passed the British Embassy I saw a great crowd carrying banners and placards coming across the Troitsky Bridge from the St. Petersburg side. I walked on. On the French Quay I was overtaken by a car with armed soldiers both inside and lying on the front mudguards with their rifles aimed forward. The same stupid, vacant, animal faces that we all remembered from the February days . . . An armoured car hurtled past in the same direction. When I got to the premises of the Central Committee, I met a woman clerk in the Secretariat and learned from her that the meeting was not there but in the Furshtadtskaya; she gave me the number. I set off for the Furshtadtskaya. At the corner of the Shpalernaya and Litejnaya it was difficult to move. There was a solid mass of people, there was ugly shouting, and an armed mass of workers was moving from the Litejnaya, then turning left along the Shpalernaya toward the Tavrichesky Palace and the Smol'ny. The placards bore Bolshevik slogans: "Down with the capitalist Ministers", "All power to the Soviets", etc. The people looked sullen and malicious. I went along Litejnaya to Furshtadtskaya, but when I arrived at the house to which I had been directed, I concluded that I had evidently been given the wrong address. I had to return to the French Quay, clear up the misunderstanding, and then return again to Furshtadtskaya once I had the right address. The meeting was in an apartment in a large building with two main entrances. Quite a large number of the Central Committee members were there. Miliukov was in the chair. A plan to appeal to the populace was being discussed. The discussion was somehow listless. People were continually going into the next room, the phone kept ringing, there were many side remarks. The meeting had been running for more than an hour when a message was brought to say that an armoured car had driven up to the building and that the way out to the street had been occupied by soldiers. This news gave rise to a lively discussion as to whether Miliukov and Shingarev* ought not to be hidden somehow and somewhere, perhaps taken out the back way or to another apartment. But they both said they would stay if their presence was no embarrassment to the owners of the apartment. The meeting went on and the discussion ended without incident. I think Miliukov and Shingarev passed the night there. It turned out that the armoured car had left and the exit was clear. It was after 11 o'clock, sultry and dusty. I had a long way to go. I decided to go along Litejnaya and Pantelejmonovskaya, past the Summer Park and the Field of Mars to the Mojka and across the Palace Square straight to St. Isaac's. In spite of the late hour, traffic in Litejnaya was as in daytime. Knots of people were constantly forming, soldiers and sailors were walking about with rifles, and cars were hooting. It got quieter and more deserted near the Field of Mars. I went my way without incident of any kind and, reaching Voznesensky Avenue (along Admiralty Avenue), I turned left. A small group of worried guests was standing outside the Hotel Anglia and among them was my cousin Katya D., who told me that troops were on Morskaya, along the square (Mariinskaya), and in the streets, and that it was unlikely I would be allowed through. However, I made my way past

*Shingarev had just resigned from the Provisional Government together with Manuilov.

Myatlev's house and the German Embassy to Morskaya and went through without hindrance. The troops were stationed in two long ranks and were occupying Morskaya about as far as the Italian Embassy. Evidently these troops had been summoned by the government to guard the Mariinsky Palace.

My memory of the next few days is vague. The appearance of the town changed quickly. Private cars disappeared, armoured and other cars roared along the streets, crammed with armed workers and soldiers. Now and then an exchange of fire would erupt in various places, and the crackle of shots would start up from various directions. People crowding the pavements on the Nevsky Prospect would suddenly leap to one side and flee in a headlong rush, nearly knocking over those who were coming toward them. Sometimes large detachments would appear, marching off somewhere and carrying red banners and placards with the slogans I've mentioned. The days were beautiful and hot, the sun shone, there was a striking contrast between nature and the alarming, disturbing things that were happening. The Mariinsky Palace was deserted, hardly anyone turned up at the meetings of the commission. I walked about the streets, visited the offices of *Rech'*, and tried to get a clear picture of events. Prince L'vov and some of the Ministers were in the District Headquarters (in the Palace Square). It was said that an unsuccessful attempt to arrest the Provisional Government had been made on the first day. Everybody was nervously waiting for something to happen. . . The whole affair ended, as we know, with the arrival from the front of troops (a Cavalry Division) loyal to the government, the rebels were cut off and disarmed, the government won a complete victory, and Bolshevism was, only temporarily, alas, routed. This was the occasion which the Provincial Government could have turned to good account to eliminate Lenin and his band once and for all. But it did not decide to do so. The new government statement contained only new concessions to Socialism and Zimmerwaldism, then Prince L'vov left his post, and then Kerensky took control of the government. . .

After the July crisis, the formation of the new Cabinet, the summoning of the Moscow State Conference, the Kornilov affair, and the temporary activity of the so-called "Directory", the setting up of the Council of the Russian Republic and the invitation to representatives of trade and industry (Tret'yakov, Smirnov, Konovalov) and also to prominent Kadets (Kishkin) to enter the government were a last attempt to check the growing wave of Bolshevism. I was taking an active part in this final phase of the Provisional Government's existence. Miliukov and Vinaver took part in only a few episodes belonging to this period. When it turned out that Tsereteli, who had played the most prominent part (on behalf of the Socialists) in the negotiations, was going off to the Caucasus and would not be at the meetings of the Council, I asked him whom we should deal with in party negotiations and agreements. He named F. Dan (Gurvich).

As is known, in the establishment of the Council of the Russian Republic the coalition parties (mainly the Socialists and the Kadets) pursued a definite aim, which was to reinforce the Provisional Government in its fight with Bolshevism. It was necessary to clear the air, to give the government a platform from which it could speak officially and openly before the whole country, and to get genuine support for it from the parties which were represented in the coalition. This required above all, of course, a firm and clear unanimity of all the parties on two counts: the fight against Bolshevism and support of the government. When the job of appointing the members of the Council of the Russian Republic was completed, Adzhemov and I came to an arrangement with Gotz, Dan, and Skobelev and agreed to meet (in Adzhemov's apartment) to work out the details and draw up a tactical plan.

If I am not mistaken, we met about twice at Adzhemov's place, and I vividly remember the discouragement and irritation that gradually came over me during these discussions. I hardly knew Dan, whom I had met in 1906 and had not seen since. His attitude to the state of affairs that was developing bore little resemblance to Tsereteli's. In answer to Adzhemov's and my clear statement that we considered that the newly constituted Council's main task was to create an atmosphere of public confidence around the Provisional Government and to support it in its fight with the Bolsheviks, Dan said that he and his friends were not disposed to promise their confidence and support in advance, that everything would depend on the government's line of action, and

99

that, in particular, they could not envisage adopting the position that the Bolsheviks must be combatted first and foremost and at all cost . . . "But look here, that was the whole point of our agreement", we retorted, "and now your attitude is once again the old uncertain, faltering, wavering, 'up-to-a-point' confidence, which is no help whatever to the government and doesn't make its task any easier." Dan tried to wriggle out of it; he hummed and hawed and put forth some doctrinaire arguments. . . We disbanded with heavy hearts, knowing that the old procrastination had begun again, that our "friends on the Left" were incorrigible, and that all our efforts to get an agreement and support for the government in its fight with anarchy and sedition had virtually been wasted.

In the end, as we know, that is how it turned out. The Provisional Government did not have the support of a definite and reliable majority in the Council of the Russian Republic. The conspicuous withdrawal of the Bolsheviks was, as I see it, of decisive importance, because after that the internationalists, who were fairly closely connected with the rest of the Socialist morass, had to fill the role of extreme Left. The Council proved to be a very cumbersome machine, and a lot of time was spent organizing it and making it function. The Board of Elders could easily have been called the Sanhedrim. The overwhelming majority were Jews. The only Russians were Avksent'ev, myself, Peshekhonov, and Chajkovsky. . . I remember that my attention was drawn to this fact by Mark Vishnyak who, as Secretary, was sitting beside me (I was Deputy Chairman).

It emerged in the preliminary negotiations that Avksent'ev was appointed Chairman, Peshekhonov, Krokhmal', and myself Deputy Chairmen, and Vishnyak Secretary. I hadn't known Avksent'ev before, but his muddled and inane speech at the Moscow Conference (which he made as Minister of Internal Affairs), had made a very unfavourable impression on me. Closer acquaintance during October and November changed this impression. Avksent'ev is a very attractive person, undoubtedly sincere and quite without conceit, and he realized that Russia was on the brink of a precipice. As Chairman of the Council he behaved impeccably and was both polite and pleasant in his personal dealings. For all

100

that, however, he was the very last person whom one would call outstanding and strong, capable of winning the respect of others and persuading them to follow him. As Chairman he showed complete objectivity and impartiality, but, of course, it was difficut for him in one month or less to gain any authority.

One of our party's practical tasks in the Council was to secure the removal of General Verkhovsky from the post of War Minister. From the very outset he had appeared as a somewhat enigmatic figure, utterly unsound, a sort of disturbed type, undeserving of any trust. At the Conference Adzhemov spoke first, very strongly and vehemently, against Verkhovsky, then came K. N. Sokolov (using information supplied to him by Adzhemov). Some time later—it must have been in the second week of October —when I departed one morning from Avksent'ev's study, where a meeting of the Presidium was in progress, and reached the Council's conference room, I found Shingarev, Miliukov, and Adzhemov in discussion. They told me that a messenger from General Verkhovsky had come to the Mariinsky Palace to say that he would like to discuss serious matters with the leaders of the Kadet Party and, if they agreed, requested them to specify any neutral place where they could meet. We suggested to Verkhovsky that he should come to the Mariinsky Palace, but he telephoned to say that he would prefer a less conspicuous place. Then the choice fell on my house on Morskaya. The appointment was set for 2 P.M. I think that, apart from the Kadets named above, F. F. Kokoshkin also was present. Verkhovsky arrived punctually, accompanied by his adjutant. We arranged ourselves in a circle in my study. Verkhovsky plunged *in medias res* and said that he would like to hear the opinion of the leaders of the Kadet Party as to whether immediate steps, including influencing our Allies, should be taken toward peace negotiations. Then he began to give reasons for his proposal and painted a picture, with which in part we were familiar, of the collapse of the Army, the desperate situation with regard to provisions and supplies in general, losses in horses, and the complete failure of communications. His conclusion was as follows: "In these conditions we cannot go on fighting and any attempts to continue the war only bring disaster nearer."

101

My position was psychologically a very difficult one. Only a month before I had been present at a private conference called by Prince Grigorij Nikolaevich Trubetskoj to discuss this same question. Tereshchenko and Neratov were at the meeting and of those who had been invited I remember Rodzyanko, Konovalov, Tret'yakov (the latter two were already ministers), Savich (a member of the State Duma), Mikhail Stakhovich, Maklakov, P. B. Struve, Baron B. E. Nol' de; I think that is all. Miliukov was not there, because he was away from St. Petersburg at the time. The question was reduced essentially to whether the situation at the moment warranted a move toward peace and whether our military situation required such a move.

For a long time before this conference I had repeatedly and with evergrowing alarm given this question considerable thought. Once, quite by chance, I had occasion to discuss the matter with Tereshchenko in the Winter Palace and tell him my fears. As a matter of fact he shared them, but he still maintained that, according to General Alekseev, the army could yet be saved and reorganized and the spring campaign prepared, and that for the time being we must and could hold the front. I must admit that his ideas far from convinced me. When later, chiefly at the initiative of Baron Nol'de and Adzhemov, the question was raised in our Central Committee (this must have been in the last week of September and also in Miliukov's absence), Baron Nol'de made a comprehensive report, the gist of which was this: the longer the war went on, the greater and more irretrievable our losses would be; our army was more and more a prey to Bolshevism; from the pattern of events it could already be foreseen that the war would end in a stalemate without a clearcut victory for either side; and we must make every effort to persuade our Allies to open peace negotiations since a seperate peace was naturally out of the question.

The overwhelming majority of members of the Central Committee were unfavorably impressed by the report and the ideas expounded in it. As far as I remember it was defended only by A. A. Dobrovol'sky (firmly and decidely) and by myself. No resolutions were passed, and it was decided to await Miliukov's return and then reconsider anew the subject of the war and foreign policy. Such a discussion, by the way, never took place. Miliukov did not

102

return until 10 October (after our Moscow Congress), and within a few weeks the Bolshevik revolution took place.

At the conference at Trubetskoj's Baron Nol'de repeated his argument more or less word for word. This time, too, he generally failed to win any sympathy. M. V. Rodzyanko made a strongly worded objection, and Savich and others also argued against the case. The substance of the objections consisted partly in a denial of the total and irrevocable demoralization of our army and partly in showing that we had no reason at all to expect our Allies to be well disposed to peace negotiations. Here, too, I supported Nol'de. A. I. Konovalov also committed himself to Nol'de's conclusions with considerable fervour and candour. I recall that he said that the government which brought Russia peace would achieve enormous popularity and become extremely powerful.

I had to leave before the meeting ended, and I did not hear Struve's and Maklakov's speeches, but, as I was told later, only the latter gave Nol'de some support. It was decided to meet periodically to exchange views, but there was no second meeting.

It goes without saying that at our meeting with Verkhovsky my position was different from what it had been in the Central Committee and at Trubetskoj's conference. Verkhovsky was consulting us as leaders of the Kadets. Miliukov and Shingarev were, of course, the most authoritative among us. They at once attacked Verkhovsky. I had to keep quiet, all the more so because his weakness was too obvious, and it was impossible to expect any systematic and successful activity from him in this most complex and delicate matter. Once again his whole personality produced a markedly unfavourable impression. It was to be feared that, if left to take the initiative alone, he could get us into a hopeless mess. Moreover, his recent political past was so murky that one could not disregard the possibility that he might be playing right into the hands of the Bolsheviks. The talk ended with Verkhovsky asking: "So I cannot count on your support in this direction?" On being told that this was the case, he rose and took his leave, but on the next day at the evening session of a commission of the Council of the Russian Republic (a military affairs commission), he repeated his whole thesis in amplified form, together with the same conclusions. It was then that he clashed with Tereshchenko, who asked him point-blank (and he received the answer "yes"): "Can you, Verkhovsky, confirm that what you have said is being said for the first time at this meeting of the commission, and that there has been no discussion of the matter in the government?" Verkhovsky replied that he really had not hitherto made this report to the Provisional Government. This made a quite scandalous impression. Verkhovsky was sent on leave with the understanding that he would not be returning. A few days later, the Bolshevik revolution took place.

During those October days, Kishkin, Kartashov, and Tret'yakov, who was allied with them, together with the Central Committee and myself, met daily after 5 o'clock at No. 10 Admiralty Quay, a house very well known to me, in the former apartment of my father-in-law which then was occupied by A. G. Khrushchyov. The object of these meetings was, firstly, to keep Ministers in constant communication with the Central Committee and, secondly, to provide them with reliable and accurate information about everything that was happening in the government. . . At these meetings of ours Konovalov always looked depressed and seemed to have lost all hope. "Ah! my dear Vladimir Dmitrievich, it's bad, very bad!" I well remember these words of his inasmuch as he said them to me many times (he was especially trusting and benevolent toward me). It was Kerensky in particular who depressed him. By this time he had become totally disillusioned with Kerensky and had no more confidence in him. What chiefly made him despair was Kerensky's inconstancy, the fact that it was quite impossible to take him at his word, his susceptibility to all sorts of influences and pressure from the outside, sometimes even the most fortuitous. "It happens like this quite often, almost every day", he would say. "You arrange everything, you insist on some measure or other, you get agreement at last. 'Yes, yes, Aleksandr Fyodorovich, it's now hard and fast, it's decided once and for all, there will be no change.' You get an absolute assurance. You leave his office, and within a few hours you hear that a completely different decision is already being put into effect, or, at best, that an urgent measure which had to be adopted at once, no later than today, is again being delayed, because new doubts have arisen or old ones which you thought had been dispelled have been resur-

104

rected. And so it is day after day. There is really no end to it." He and all of us were worried by the military situation in St. Petersburg and the part played by Colonel Polkovnikov, in whom Konovalov had not a grain of confidence. In those days Kerensky was evidently going through a period of despondency. It was quite impossible to make him adopt any rigorous measures, time was passing, and the Bolsheviks were exerting themselves to the fullest and standing less and less on ceremony. The situation was grimmer every day. Rumours that the Bolshevik uprising would come within a few days were circulating and they worried and alarmed everyone. During those days the—purely academic—order for Lenin's arrest was issued.

The day before the Bolshevik revolution, Kerensky, as we know, appeared in the Council of the Russian Republic, announced the exposure of a plot, and asked for support and plenary powers. By chance I was not in the Mariinsky Palace at the time. I arrived a little later and came upon a scene of utter confusion. The usual painful process—which in these circumstances was particularly remarkable for its paltriness and irrelevancy—was underway: the search for a compromise which might be acceptable to some non-existent majority. In the end the Kadets did not put forward their own formula, having decided to associate themselves with the National Socialists and the Syndicalists, but the latter were by no means voting as a solid block and, as a consequence, when the vote was taken by their passage through the doorway, there was no majority. At the crucial moment the council of the Republic had proved wanting. It had not given the government moral support but, on the contrary, had dealt it a moral blow by revealing the government's isolation. I will not claim that a diffent vote would have delayed the course of events for any length of time or would have stopped the Bolsheviks, but the outcome of this grievous and shameful day could only have raised the Bolsheviks' morale, filled them with hope, and added to their resolve. On the other hand, this day shed a glaring light on the negative features of our "revolutionary democracy"—its shortsighted stupidity, its fanaticism for words and formulas, and its lack of any aptitude for governing. No genuine, strong, reasonable government could have functioned with its intrinsic features. We dispersed in a mood of extreme depression.

The next day, sometimes between 9 and 10 A.M., while I was in my dressing room, a servant knocked and told me that two officers wished to see me. I asked her to show them into the study and joined them there a few minutes later. These officers (one, as far as I remember, a Staff Captain; the other, a lieutenant) were unknown to me. They looked very worried. The senior of the two stated his name and position and said: "I expect you are aware that the rebellion has started; postal, telegraph, and telephone services, the arsenal and stations have been seized. All the main centres are in the hands of the Bolsheviks. The troops are defecting to them, and there is no resistance. The Provisional Government is finished. Our task is to save Kerensky and drive him as soon as possible to the troops which have remained loyal to the government and which are marching on Luga. All our vehicles have been confiscated or are out of service. We have come to ask you whether you can provide two closed cars or tell us where we can get them. Every minute counts now." I was so taken aback that for a moment I thought it might be a trick to obtain a car and drive it away. I asked where Kerensky was. The officer told me he was at District Headquarters in Polkovnikov's office. I asked two or three more questions, and then I had to explain to the officers that I had only an old, not very powerful, battered Benz landaulet for driving around town, which was absolutely no good for what they wanted, and I was hard put to suggest any other cars, since, because of all the requisitioning, both before and after the revolution, none of my friends possessed cars of the sort required. So I was unable to help. The officers left at once, saying that they would go and look elsewhere. Having shown them out, I warned my wife of what was happening and soon afterward left the house and went to the Mariinsky Palace, where the Presidium of the Council of the Russian Republic met every morning between 10 and 11 o'clock. There were already quite a few people there. The atmosphere everywhere was one of bewilderment, anxiety, and helplessness. The Social-Republican group was absent entirely, and only a few Social-Democrats were present. Avksent'ev did not know what to do. There were too few members to start the meeting, but, most importantly, all his own group was absent. After a fairly long wait, the members of the Council who were present began to grow restive and demanded either that the meeting be started or that an announcement that it would not take place be made. Then Avksent'ev called the Senior Committee together to decide to what to do. At this moment the Council's constable reported that Kerensky had just driven across the square in the direction of Voznesensky Avenue in an open (sic!) car with two adjutants and followed by a second, closed car. Where the other members of the Provisional Government were and what they were doing nobody knew . . . The Senior Committee met. A very short time after the meeting got underway E. D. Kuskova (who was not a member of the Senior Committee) asked permission to come in and reported that a detachment of troops led by an officer had arrived, that all the exits to the square were blocked, and that the officer wished to see the Chairman. The answer given was the Chairman was busy, that a meeting of the Board of Elders was in progress, and that, when it was finished, it would be possible to see him. Some time later Kuskova again appeared and gave the message that the commander of the detachment advised all those at the meeting and all members of the Council, to leave the Mariinsky Palace at once, otherwise vigorous steps, not excluding the use of firearms, would be taken. This had a staggering effect. Evidently no one was tempted by the prospect of dying for the glory of the Council of the Russian Republic, and there was no impulse to recall famous historical precedents, since the Council of the Republic was a purely fortuitous, *ad hoc* body in no way commensurate with a national government. There was absolutely no ideological motive for defending it at all costs. It was very clearly felt that the situation of the Council was closely linked with the situation of the Provisional Government. In answer to the ultimatum, a routine resolution was quickly drafted about force used against the Council in which it was said that the Council would be summoned again at the first opportunity. I think somebody suggested gathering all the members of the Council who were present in the general assembly hall, but this motion was not passed because the number of members was dwindling quickly, and no enthusiastic demonstration was to be expected. When we

107

went into the antechamber which adjoined the general assembly hall, the staircase and first anteroom upstairs were occupied by armed soldiers and sailors. They were in two ranks on both sides of the stairs. The usual inane, stupid, and malevolent faces. I do not think any one of them could have told you why he was there, who had sent him, and who we were. I was walking with Miliukov. I wanted to make sure he left the Palace unhindered. In the big entrance hall downstairs was a large crowd of soldiers and sailors also drawn up in ranks as far as the door. The driveway outside was occupied and a naval officer was letting people out. Everyone going out was showing his identity card. Thinking that this was for identification purposes and under specific orders, I felt quite sure that Miliukov and I would be arrested. We were walking in single file. I was in front of him. Just before I went out the door, there was some obstruction in the driveway, and everything came to a halt. Two or three agonizing minutes passed. As at all such moments I have experienced in my life, I felt only a heightening of nerves, nothing more. They let us out. I thought that the officer hesitated when he glanced at Miliukov's card, but it all happened very quickly, and we both found ourselves out in the square. I invited him to my house for lunch, but he told me he preferred to go home, and we shook hands and parted. It was not until 1918, from 10 to 23 June, that we met again in Kiev, after a nightmare of seven and a half months . . .

After I came home, I stayed there for a time and at about 3 o'clock went to visit a friend who lived on the Fontanka near the corner of Voznesensky Avenue. At about 4 o'clock I telephoned my home to find out if there was any news. My wife told me that a messenger, a newspaper man, had just come from A. I. Konovalov with an urgent request for me to go to the Winter Palace where members of the Council of the Russian Republic and Representatives of other public bodies were meeting. A session of the Provisional Government would apparently be held there in normal conditions, under military guard. I was surprised at this unexpected summons, but, it goes without saying, I decided to comply with it. I caught a tram on Pod'yacheskaya, went as far as Konnogvardejsky Avenue, changed trams, and proceeded to the Palace square. The square was cordoned off. Thin ranks of soldiers were stationed along the drive, parallel to the Aleksandrovsky Gardens, around the square, and along the railings of the Palace grounds. Many people crowded the pavements. It was hard to know what was happening and what the significance of the troops was. Keeping my habit of not asking questions on such occassions, I took out my pass to the Winter Palace (I had used the pass when I attended meetings of the Provisional Government), showed it without a word to the first soldier I met, and he let me through with no difficulty. I passed freely through the gate and entered the Palace by the usual way, the Saltykovsky entrance, went up the stairs and to the Malakhitov hall. There I found the following scene: all the Ministers were present except N. M. Kishkin (who was in the District Headquarters building in the Palace square "organizing" the defence, with, as we know, pathetic results). Konovalov looked extremely worried. The Ministers were in groups, some pacing up and down, others standing by the window; S. N. Tret'yakov sat beside me on a settee and indignantly told me that Kerensky had deserted and betrayed them and that the situation was hopeless. Others were saying (I remember a very tense and excited Tereshchenko) that they had only to persevere for forty-eight hours and the loyal government troops who were marching toward St. Petersburg would arrive. My arrival was very welcome. It transpired that Konovalov had sent messengers in all directions summoning "vital forces" prepared to rally round the government. A few of the messengers had been stopped by the Bolsheviks, but the others had reached their destinations and passed on the invitation. However, no one aside from me had answered the call. It need hardly be said that my presence proved to be utterly useless. I was unable to help in any way, and, when it became clear that the Provisional Government had no intention of doing anything and was adopting a passive, "wait and see" attitude, I decided to leave, at the point when Konovalov was told that dinner was served (just after 6 o'clock). In the corridor I encountered some journalists led by L. M. Klyachko-L'vov. They told me they intended to stay with the Provisional Government to the end. In point of fact they did not stay long after me and had difficulty leaving the Palace, but I walked out quite freely and went home. About fifteen minutes after I left, all exits and gates were blocked by the Bolsheviks, and they did not let anybody else through. Thus it was that only a lucky chance stopped me from sharing the fate of the Provisional Government and the subsequent ordeals which ended in the Peter-Paul fortress.

I spent the evening of that tempestuous day, I remember, at home. At about 2 o'clock the next day I went to the City Duma. Our Central Committee had met in the morning at Countess S. V. Panina's house, and it continued to meet daily during the next ten or fifteen days, either at Panina's or V. A. Stepanov's and once at Kutler's—the day the Kadets tried to seize the telephone exchange. The City Duma met every day during the day, and in the evenings the Committee for Saving the Country and the Revolution, which was formed immediately after the revolution and used the premises of the Peasants' Union, was now holding its meetings in the College of Law.

At the time the City Duma resembled a huge, disturbed anthill. All the halls, rooms, lobbies, and staircases were teeming with people. There was nobody one did not meet there. But, alas, one was able to indulge only momentarily in the illusion that the City Duma, together with the Committee for Saving the Country and Revolution, might become an organized centre of resistance to the Bolsheviks. It very soon became obvious that they had no real organized power. Among my most painful memories is the visit Avksent'ev and I and, as I recall, Shrejder (the mayor) and Isaev (the chairman of the City Duma) paid to the British ambassador, Buchanan. This was on the day after the revolt. The purpose of the visit was to "set the ambassador's mind at rest" and assure him that the success of the Bolshevik rebellion was purely illusory and specious, that Kerensky was bringing an army corps to rescue St. Petersburg and the Provisional Government. . . Heaven alone knows to what extent we ourselves believed these soothing words. Buchanan, whom I had met before my trip to England in January 1916 in the same study where he now received us, was upset and depressed. The conversation flagged, particularly because Avksent'ev had difficulty expressing himself in French. On mention of the eagerly awaited army corps the ambassador brightened somewhat. This useless visit left me with a feeling of disgust. I recalled the alluring speeches at the Provisional Government's reception for ambassadors in the Mariinsky Palace, speeches ringing with confidence in the power of the government and the greatness of the revolution, and I instinctively juxtaposed that moment, which was not far in the past, with the disgraceful experiences of the Bolshevik *coup de main*. As we know, the next few days revealed the utter futility of placing hopes on a military force and ended with the rout of Krasnov's Cossacks and with Kerensky's flight.

The meetings of the City Duma were nothing but hysterical outbursts. The tone was set by the mayor, G. I. Shrejder, in many respects an estimable person but apparently without inhibitory centres. The ridiculous All-Russian Assembly of District Councils which he convened allegedly in implementation of a City Duma resolution (in fact, the debate was chaotic; only something like a wish was expressed), proved an utter failure; nothing else could have been expected in the circumstances. The Bolsheviks probably treated this attempt "to organize public opinion" with great irony and went on with their own, very practical, business. The daily meeting of the Duma was just like an ordinary rally. There was no agenda, no order of procedure. It was all done in the form of urgent, pressing, extraordinary statements. Usually the mayor himself made them. Immediately afterward a stormy debate would begin. The bulk of the Bolsheviks stopped attending the meetings after the rebellion, but they left representatives such as the city councillor, Kobozev, a disgusting character, and a few others. These gentlemen first tried to give as good as they got in abuse, then they generally sat silent, and after a time they, too, stopped attending the meetings. Poor A. I. Shingarev played first fiddle in our group. He kept making impassioned speeches, invariably calling the Bolsheviks traitors and murderers. Alas, we had no means of knowing that these speeches were his swan song. . . A little later Vinaver arrived from Moscow where he had been when the rebellion took place. But I do not remember that he made any outstanding speeches at this time.

The Kadet group in the City Duma delegated Countess S. V. Panina, Prince V. A. Obolensky, and myself to form part of the Committee for saving the Country and the Revolution. We attended these meetings very regularly, especially in the beginning, when it still seemed that some effective force might polarize around the Committee on something of that order. But our position on the Committee was a rather peculiar one. Its membership was, *ex professo*, "democratic" in that special sense which excludes all non-Socialist elements from the concept of "democracy". None of us, therefore, formed part of the Committee's Bureau. However, any real committee work was done in the Bureau. It was the Bureau that organized the military coup (by the Junkers) which had such a tragic end. The Committee itself was concerned with resolutions, and there were usually arguments about every phrase, every single word, as though the salvation of "the Country and the Revolution" depended on such phrases and words. The attendance kept dwindling, the pointlessness and futility of the meetings became more and more obvious . . . The days immediately following the rebellion passed in this manner. In the morning, there were meetings of the Central Committee, discussions, so-called "briefings" at which at least half of the information was unconfirmed rumours and fantastic stories; then there would be long, wearisome, and utterly useless debates ending with the approval of the draft of some appeal or with a totally unnecessary resolution. The 15 or 20 people who met together were only too keenly and clearly aware of their complete powerlessness, their isolation, the lack of any organization which might support them. There was this awareness in both the City Duma and the Committee for Saving the Country and the Revolution . . .

It seemed at first as though the possibility of an electoral campaign of any sort for the Constituent Assembly was quite out of the question. I myself, I remember, expressed this opinion both in the Central Committee and the All-Russian Electoral Commission. The latter body decided to suspend its work temporarily and in fact did not meet for approximately two weeks. Everyone expected the Bolsheviks to start a campaign against the Constituent Assembly. They proved to be more cunning. As we know, in their first manifesto they accused the Provisional Government of delaying the elections to the Constituent Assembly and for the first month after the rebellion they made a great show of their desire to convene it. Only once they felt their own strength, or better, when they felt sure of the opposition's impotence, did they

112

open their campaign, at first cautiously, then openly and flagrantly. They did not obstruct the electoral campaign in St. Petersburg during November. The first meeting organized by our party was fixed, if I am not mistaken, for Sunday, 5 November. A. I. Shingarev was supposed to speak. We expected Bolshevik demonstrations, heckling, and so on. Nothing of the sort happened. As is usually the case, the meeting attracted an audience exclusively of Kadets or Kadet sympathisers; it was held in the Tenishev School in the Litejny district, that Kadet stronghold, and it was, as was reported, a very lively one. After that there was a series of meetings in St. Petersburg and its environs. I spoke in the Tenishev School, in the hall of the Kalashnikov Exchange, in a high school on Kazanskaya, in Luga, and in Petergof. I also spoke by special invitation in the hall of the General Staff (for the staff) and at the Salamander Society (for the employees). There may have been other speeches, too, which I cannot now recall. The representatives of the other (Socialist) parties hardly spoke at these meetings, while the Bolsheviks kept away altogether. The mood of the audience was, on the whole, one of alarm and despondency . . .

At one of the first sessions of the Committee for Saving the Country and the Revolution, Countess S. V. Panina told me that my presence was requested at a session of Deputy Ministers of the Provisional Government to be held at A. A. Dem'yanov's house on Bassejnaya. If I am not mistaken, I attended only one session (the first), and I recollect it with extreme distaste. It was a gathering of people who had completely lost their heads. Also present at the meeting, apart from Deputy Ministers, were three Socialist Ministers who had been released by the Bolsheviks from the Peter-Paul fortress during the first few days. When they (Nikitin, Malyantovich, and Gvozdev) came into the room, Dem'yanov tried to "greet them with applause", but no one supported him. More sensitive people realized that there was nothing to applaud. The Socialist Ministers were released in circumstances that by no means did them credit. One would have thought, when they were told that they were free to go but that the other, "bourgeois" Ministers were remaining in the fortress, that a simple sense of comradely solidarity would have caused them to object vigorously to such discrimination (an absurdity emphasized by the fact that the head of the Provisional Government was, after all, a Socialist), and that they would have protested, not in words and written statements alone, but practically and effectively by refusing the freedom offered them under these conditions. If only they had been turned out of the fortress by force; naturally, one can't do anything about force. But to leave as they did was ethically wrong, and I can well understand how, when Konovalov was told how they had left, he was quite distraught. As if to complete the picture, one of the Ministers (I think it was Gvozdev) thought it proper and necessary to ask to see M. I. Tereshchenko, in order to "consult" with him and inquire how he and the other Ministers remaining in the fortress felt about the release of the Socialists! What could poor Tereshchenko say to that? Naturally, he said that they should avail themselves of the Bolsheviks' kindness, but he was unable to hide his feelings completely and was evidently quite despondent, too, as whoever it was who went to see him reported himself . . . Needless to say, there was no dearth of plausible excuses to explain the conduct of the Socialist Ministers. They were said to have walked out in order to "carry on the fight", in order to preserve the appearance of the "machinery of government", and, first and foremost, in order to try to obtain the release of the other members of the Provisional Government. In fact, it immediately became clear that they were powerless in all these matters. A. M. Nikitin, evidently the most sensitive of them, was obviously very upset by their position. At the session I attended, he very excitedly interrupted Gvozdev, asking Gvozdev to accompany him to Smol'ny and, "stopping at nothing", demand categorically the release of the imprisoned Ministers and, in the event of a refusal, to insist that those who had been released be put back in prison! . . . However, Gvozdev showed not the slightest desire to do this, and the others who were there—mainly Dem'yanov—tried to show Nikitin that his plan was fanciful and impracticable, that the thing to do was to "look after" the fragments of the Provisional Government . . . In the end, Nikitin abandoned his plan.

The Nikitin episode is my clearest memory of the meeting. It was all very confused, and, as chairman Dem'yanov did not know how to put questions or keep a debate to the point, there was the usual verbiage, the endless speeches to which no one listened. The general mood was terrible, and some, especially Gvozdev, seemed to be in a panic. I think only one specific means of fighting was discussed, a strike of officials, and it must be said that this strike and the foolishly heroic action of the Junkers were the only evidence of practical resistance to the Bolsheviks.

After that, I did not attend these meetings any more, inasmuch as my official position in the Provisional Government certainly did not entitle me to be present, and I personally viewed them with complete distaste.

As regards the electoral campaign in progress, the All-Russia Electoral Commission decided, about three weeks after the rebellion, to join the Secretariat for a plenary session in the Mariinsky Palace, from which the Bolshevik guard both inside and out had then been removed, in order to discuss whether it should resume its work or not. Apart from the political uncertainties, this raised also serious legal doubts. It was clearly foreseen that, in the conditions under which the electoral campaign was to be run and the elections held, many of the requirements in the electoral law (concerning times, the composition of commissions, and so on) could not be observed. In such cases, earlier, before the rebellion, the All-Russia Commission had made appropriate representations to the Provisional Government, with a draft decree allowing legal deviation from a general law in a specific instance. The Bolshevik rebellion removed this possibility, because the Provisional Government had, in fact, been overthrown, and the All-Russia Commission could not recognize the Soviet government which had been formed. Therefore, where it proved impossible in practice to observe the time limits laid down by law, or to compose an electoral commission with the membership required by law, a hopeless situation arose. By virtue of its position, the All-Russia Commission could work only in conjunction with a government. These considerations guided us, when, immediately after the rebellion, we decided to terminate the Commission, after we had ensured that the Secretariat and the documents would be preserved. It should not be forgotten that at that time no one, and we were no exception, believed that the Bolshevik regime would last; everyone expected that it would quickly be swept away. Quite apart from these considerations, the general confusion and chaos which followed the rebellion interrupted the work of all electoral bodies and brought to a halt—temporarily, at least—the activity of the All-Russia Commission which was directly concerned with them.

However, days passed, and the situation began to change in the sense that the All-Russia Commission's inactivity could easily have been interpreted as malicious intent to delay the elections or "sabotage" them. Telegrammes were coming from the provinces with enquiries about what was to be done, whether the elections would be held, what directives were to guide local electoral bodies. On the other hand, the Bolshevik "government", which had impudently accused the Provisional Government of intending to "drag out" the elections, was itself supposedly preparing to promote the convening of the Constituent Assembly at the appointed time, that is, 28 November. All these factors prompted the Commission to reconsider the question of its future activity. With this aim in mind it was decided to hold a meeting.

When I arrived at the Mariinsky Palace on the appointed day, I found very worried Secretariat officials. Apparently N. N. Avinov, the chairman of the Commission, had departed urgently and unexpectedly for Moscow, and the duties of chairman had been passed on to me. The first thing I had to do, as chairman, was to talk with representatives of the Soviet of People's Commissars, their Head of Secretariat, Bonch-Bruevich, and some soldier or other, who had come on the instructions of that body. According to the Secretariat officials, these two persons had arrived at the Palace, enquired of the whereabouts of the All-Russia Commission and, once they were given directions, they had made their way to the Secretariat and demanded to see the clerical work and to be informed about the Commission's activities. They had been told that the Deputy Chairman, who was standing in for the Chairman, was due to arrive soon, and they were requested to wait and talk with me.

I knew Bonch-Bruevich slightly, having met him in Kiev in the autumn of 1913 in the Bejlis case.[11] At that time he was very respectful. If I am not mistaken, I dined with him at S. V. Glinka's home. As we discussed only the Bejlis case then, I could not form any further impression of Bonch-Bruevich himself. As I discovered later, he became head of the Secretariat of the Soviet of Commissars through the influence of Steklov-Nakhamkes and was one of Steklov's minions. Bramson told me he had a very unsavoury reputation and was considered a crook. His role in the rise of the newspaper *Novaya Zhizn'* was a decidedly murky one, according to A. I. Konovalov. Here in the Mariinsky Palace he greeted me like an old friend, was pointedly polite, and said that the Soviet of People's Commissars was keenly interested in the Constituent Assembly elections and would like a clarification of the role of the All-Russia Commission. I invited him and his companion, the soldier, into the hall that was used as a tea room (adjoining the antechamber). L. M. Bramson, the second deputy chairman, came along, and we got down to business. I explained to Bonch-Bruevich the All-Russia Commission's view, which was based on non-recognition of the newly arisen authority of the "Sovnarkom".* Bonch-Bruevich tried to convince me that the basis of Bolshevik authority was just as legal, if not more so, than the Provisional Government's, but I declined to discuss the matter. I added that a meeting of the Commissars was due to begin now, at which the question of its continued activity would be discussed again. "May I hope that you will inform me of the outcome of the discussion?" I replied that officially the Commission would almost certainly not have any dealings whatsoever with the Soviet, but that I was prepared to tell him, Bonch-Bruevich, privately what decision was made, always provided that the Commission had no objection. He declared himself completely satisfied with this. The soldier who was with him took hardly any part in the conversation and only once joined in to say "on behalf of the front" that the elections were being awaited with great impatience and that everything must be done to have them. I pointed out to him in reply that it was the Bolshevik rebellion on the eve of the elections and a month before the Constituent Assembly that had dealt the elections a savage blow and made it dubious whether they could be held. With this the conversation ended and our two

---

*This vulgar term was not then in use. I call it "vulgar" by association of ideas.

visitors gone, I opened the meeting of the Commission, and after a brief debate we passed a resolution to resume the business of the Commission, ignore the Bolshevik government completely, and, if problems requiring a legal solution arose, to leave it to the local bodies to circumvent the difficulties, without, however, our sanctioning any deviation from the law. At the same time it was assumed that the Constituent Assembly, in verifying the authority of its members, would take into account the desperate situation that had arisen and regard as immaterial any deviations (mainly with regard to time limits and the composition of commissions) that local organizations had allowed. The next morning I phoned Bonch-Bruevich and gave him the following information: "Firstly, I am requested to inform you that the All-Russia Commission has resolved to ignore the Soviet of People's Commissars completely, not to recognize its legal authority, and not to have any dealings whatsoever with it. This is the end of the official part of our conversation. Privately, and in accordance with the promise I made you, I can inform you that the Commission resolved to resume its business and at once did so." Bonch-Bruevich thanked me warmly . . .

Here I must observe that the Bolshevik government evidently did not have the slightest understanding of the membership of the Commission or its functions, and apparently it assumed that the Commission would actually conduct the elections and influence their progress and outcome. At any rate, in the course of the next two or three weeks the Commission was able to work without interference. We met daily at the Mariinsky Palace, and I had to take the chair several times because of N. N. Avinov's frequent trips to Moscow. We were very busy with local bodies, scores of telegrams arrived every day which bore witness to the enormous difficulties being encountered in the provinces. For the most part, these telegrams asked the All-Russia Commission for permission to allow exceptions or deviations from the stipulations of the electoral law of one kind or another, and the Commission, being powerless to grant these requests, was forced to leave them unanswered. Apart from this, however, there were numerous cases in which we had to interpret the law and give various instructions. Subsequently, of course, a general picture of the elections,

118

albeit incomplete and fragmentary, began to emerge. After Bonch-Bruevich's visit the Soviet government ceased to take any interest in the Commission's activity. On about 20 November it was decided to transfer the clerical work and the meetings of the Commission to the Tavrichesky Palace. This was done while I was away. I left for Moscow on 19 November and returned on Wednesday, the 22nd, toward evening. When I returned, I discovered that a meeting was fixed for the morning of the 23rd in the Tavrichesky Palace. On the very day of my departure, an hour after I had left for the station, a search was carried out in my house, but the details are unknown to me to this day. On the 23rd, about two hours after the Commission had started its business, the Commandant of the Tavrichesky Palace, a Bolshevik ensign whose name I have forgotten, appeared and in the name of the Soviet of People's Commissars ordered the Commission to disband. N. N. Avinov was in the chair, and his reply, on behalf of the whole Commission, was a categorical refusal. The officer left, went to the Smol'ny for instructions, and came back with a document signed by Lenin and containing an order—very badly worded—to arrest the Kadet Electoral Commission and send its members to Smol'ny Prison.

Our imprisonment in the Smol'ny lasted five days. We spent the five days in a narrow, cramped little room with a rather low ceiling, which was reached by a short staircase leading from a lower corridor. There were from 12 to 15 of us, I don't remember exactly. About four or five went off to spend the night in another cell. "Among those present" I remember Avinov, Bramson, Baron Nol'de, Vishnyak, Gronsky, two members of the State Duma (one an Octobrist, the other a Peaceful Reconstructionist or Progressive, but I have quite forgotten their names), the editor of the Commission's Proceedings, Dobranitsky, three soldiers, representatives of the front, and V. M. Gessen, who was not arrested with us but appeared voluntarily, placed himself under arrest, and spent twenty-four hours (I think) with us and had to be turned out almost by force the following day.*

---

*Dobranitsky and the other members of the Front-Line Commission had not been arrested and were in prison at their own insistence. Attempts were also made to remove them, and they used military tricks, including disguise, to get back and join us.

We were not too well off the first day. The room contained wooden benches, chairs, two wretched beds on which our two oldest colleagues, the members of the State Duma, slept, and that was all. I slept on a rather narrow wooden bench, Vishnyak on a chair. We were not given sheets or mattresses. On the first day, too, there was no sign of food or even tea, and if Baron Nol'de's wife had not brought some provisions (she was the first to hear of what had happened and managed to get a few things together), we would have gone hungry. The second day was more organized, and we started to have our dinner in the general dining-room, families brought ample provisions, camp-beds and linen appeared, two or three more mattresses were brought, and we spent the remaining days gaily and in good spirits. Our only worry was the complete uncertainty of our fate and the menacing prospect of "the Cross".[12] We were interrogated on the very first evening; the interrogation was conducted by a certain Krasikov, a barrister of the worst type, and invariably included the following question, to which we invariably answered "no": "Do you recognize the authority of the Soviet of People's Commissars?" At the end of the interrogation I asked directly: "What is the reason for our arrest?" Back came the reply: "Refusal to recognize the authority of the People's Commissars."

At about 3 o'clock on Monday, 27 November, the day before the Constituent Assembly was due to open, a ragged sailor, a member of the Commission of Inquiry, came to our room and, "in the name of the People's Government", told us that we were released. I cannot say that this news gave me any particular joy. We realized only too well that our arrest and release were nothing but chance events in an oncoming series of calamities, that, though released today, we might tomorrow be imprisoned, perhaps in far worse conditions. Before parting we had tea and something to eat for the last time and were going to draw up a document reporting the proceedings of our interrogation and release, but then we decided to put it off to another day and to meet on Tuesday morning in the Tavrichesky Palace, gathering first in L. M. Bramson's apartment. However, certain circumstances prevented me from getting to Bramson's on time and when I did arrive my colleagues had already left for the Tavrichesky Palace.

120

I hurried after them. The nearer I drew to the Palace, the thicker the crowds became. I wanted to enter the Palace from the Tavricheskaya side, but soldiers standing at the entrance would not let me pass. When I said that I was a member of the All-Russia Electoral Commission and was going to a meeting of the Commission, they said: "See the commandant". "Where is the commandant?" "At the other entrance, on Shpalernaya." I made my way to the Shpalernaya, but it was quite impossible to pass. A dense crowd formed a wall around the railings, there was shouting and shoving. I went back to the Tavricheskaya and forced my way to another entrance, where there was a less determined soldier, and because I, on the other hand, showed great determination, I gained entry. As soon as I entered the palace, I learned of the arrest that morning, about two hours earlier, in Countess Panina's house, of the Countess herself, Shingarev, Kokoshkin, and Prince Pavel Dmitrievich Dolgorukov . . . The Commission was already in session. It appeared that the commandant had already come and ordered the Commission to disband, and armed soldiers had been brought into the room. The Commission, however, refused to disperse and went on with the meeting in the presence of the soldiers. Some time later G. I. Shrejder and two or three other members of the Constituent Assembly joined us, having heard that the Commission was being obstructed. They sent for the commandant, had heated words with him, and demanded the withdrawal of the soldiers. The commandant referred to the orders he had received from Uritsky (the Commissar of the Tavrichesky Palace) and went for further instructions from him. After a time, Uritsky arrived. I remember as though it were today the repulsive figure of that seedy individual with his hat on his head and his impudent Jewish face . . . He also ordered us to disperse and threatened the use of arms. By this time Shrejder and the other members of the Constituent Assembly had left and gone to the meeting. We demanded that Uritsky remove his hat, which he hastened to do. Further negotiations got nowhere. Uritsky left, and we continued our meeting, expecting an attempt at forcible eviction any minute. This, however, did not happen. We finished our meeting after dealing with all the business, and at about 2 o'clock we adjourned, agreeing to gather again at Bramson's house the next day and to act according to circumstances.

The following day I left the house about 10 o'clock, never dreaming that I would not cross its threshold again in 1917, nor, probably, in 1918 . . .

On the way to Bramson's I read a decree outlawing the Kadet party and ordering the arrest of its leaders. When I got to Bramson's, I was received with great excitement. They all thought I had been arrested.

The same day, at the urging of intimate friends, I decided to leave for the Crimea where my family, since mid-November, had been availing themselves of the hospitality of Countess S. V. Panina. By an incredibly lucky chance I managed to obtain a first-class sleeper to Simferopol' at the booking office. Without returning home I left that evening, giving all necessary instructions by telephone and taking with me only the bare necessities. I reached Gaspra safely on Sunday, 3 December. There I spent the whole winter, spring, and part of the summer without going anywhere, surviving both the Bolshevik capture of the Crimea and then the German invasion. On 7 June I left for Kiev, with the intention of returning to St. Petersburg. But this I failed to do, and I returned to Gaspra on 22 July after spending five and a half rather agonizing weeks in Kiev. I am ending this section of my notes on 8 October (New Style), just as news of the immensely important events in Germany and Bulgaria have reached me . . .

APPENDIX

Vladimir Nabokov's memoirs of his father. An excerpt from *Speak, Memory.*

I HAVE BEFORE ME a large bedraggled scrapbook, bound in black cloth. It contains old documents, including diplomas, drafts, diaries, identity cards, penciled notes, and some printed matter, which had been in my mother's meticulous keeping in Prague until her death there, but then, between 1939 and 1961, went through various vicissitudes. With the aid of those papers and my own recollections, I have composed the following short biography of my father.

Vladimir Dmitrievich Nabokov, jurist, publicist and statesman, son of Dmitri Nikolaevich Nabokov, Minister of Justice, and Baroness Maria von Korff, was born on 20 July 1870, at Tsarskoe Selo near St. Petersburg, and was killed by an assassin's bullet on 28 March 1922, in Berlin. Till the age of thirteen he was educated at home by French and English governesses and by Russian and German tutors; from one of the latter he caught and passed on to me the *passio et morbo aureliana.* In the autumn of 1883, he started to attend the "Gymnasium" (corresponding to a combination of American "high school" and "junior college") on the then Gagarin Street (presumably renamed in the twenties by the short-sighted Soviets). His desire to excel was overwhelming. One winter night, being behind with a set task and preferring pneumonia to ridicule at the blackboard, he exposed himself to the polar frost, with the hope of a timely sickness, by sitting in nothing but his nightshirt at the open window (it gave on the Palace Square and its moon-polished pillar); on the morrow he still enjoyed perfect health, and, undeservedly, it was the dreaded teacher who happened to be laid up. At sixteen, in May 1887, he completed the Gymnasium course,with a gold medal, and studied law at the St. Petersburg University, graduating in January 1891. He continued his studies in Germany (mainly at Halle). Thirty years later, a fellow student of his, with whom he had gone for a bicycle trip in the Black Forest, sent my widowed mother the *Madame Bovary* volume which my father had had with him at the time and on the flyleaf of which he had written "The unsurpassed pearl of French literature"—a judgment that still holds.

On 14 November (a date scrupulously celebrated every subsequent year in our anniversary-conscious family) 1897, he married Elena Ivanovna Rukavishnikov, the twenty-one-year-old daughter of a country neighbor with whom he had six children (the first was a stillborn boy).

In 1895 he had been made Junior Gentleman of the Chamber. From 1896 to 1904 he lectured on criminal law at the Imperial School of Jurisprudence (*Pravovedenie*) in St. Petersburg. Gentlemen of the Chamber were supposed to ask permission of the "Court Minister" before performing a public act. This permission my father did not ask, naturally, when publishing in the review *Pravo* his celebrated article, "The Blood Bath of Kishinev", in which he condemned the part played by the police in promoting the Kishinev pogrom of 1903. By imperial decree he was deprived of his court title in January 1905, after which he severed all connection with the Tsar's government and resolutely plunged into antidespotic politics, while continuing his juristic labors. From 1905 to 1915 he was president of the Russian section of the International Criminology Association and at conferences in Holland amused himself and amazed his audience by orally translating, when needed, Russian and English speeches into German and French and vice versa. He was eloquently against capital punishment. Unswervingly he conformed to his principles in private and public matters. At an official banquet in 1904 he refused to drink the Tsar's health. He is said to have coolly advertised in the papers his court uniform for sale. From 1906 to 1917 he co-edited with I. V. Hessen and A. I. Kaminka one of the few liberal dailies in Russia, the *Rech'* as well as the jurisprudential review *Pravo*. Politically he was a Kadet, i.e. a member of the KD (*Konstitutsionno-demokraticheskaya partiya*), later renamed more aptly the party of the People's Freedom (*partiya Narodnoy Svobodi*). With his keen sense of humor he would have been tremendously tickled by the helpless though vicious hash Soviet lexicographers have made of his opinions and achievements in their rare biographical comments on him. In 1906 he was elected to the First Russian Parliament (*Pervaya Duma*), a humane and heroic institution, predominantly liberal (but which ignorant foreign publicists, infected by Soviet propaganda, often confuse with the ancient "boyar dumas"!). There he made several splendid speeches with nationwide repercussions. When less than a year later the Tsar dissolved the Duma, a number of members, including my father (who, as a photograph taken at the Finland Station shows, carried his railway ticket tucked under the band of his hat), repaired to Vyborg for an illegal session. In May 1908, he began a prison term of three months in somewhat belated punishment for the revolutionary manifesto he and his group had issued at Vyborg. "Did V. get any 'Egerias' [Speckled Woods] this summer?" he asks in one of his secret notes from prison, which, through a bribed guard, and a faithful friend (Kaminka), were transmitted to my mother at Vyra. "Tell him that all I see in the prison yard are Brimstones and Cabbage Whites." After his release he was forbidden to participate in public elections, but (one of the paradoxes so common under the Tsars) could freely work in the bitterly liberal *Rech'*, a task to which he devoted up to nine hours a day. In 1913, he was fined by the government the token sum of one hundred rubles (about as many dollars of the present time) for his reportage from Kiev, where after a stormy trial Beylis was found innocent of murdering a Christian boy for "ritual" purposes: justice and public opinion could still prevail occasionally in old Russia; they had only five years to go. He was mobilized soon after the beginning of World War One and sent to the front. Eventually he was attached to the General Staff in St. Petersburg. Military ethics prevented him from taking an active part in the first turmoil of the liberal revolution of March 1917. From the very start, History seems to have been anxious of depriving him of a full opportunity to reveal his great gifts of statesmanship in a Russian republic of the Western type. In 1917, during the initial stage of the Provisional Government—that is, while the Kadets still took part in it—he occupied in the Council of Ministers the responsible but inconspicuous position of Executive Secretary. In the winter of 1917-18, he was elected to the Constituent Assembly, only to be arrested by energetic Bolshevist sailors when it was disbanded. The November Revolution had already entered upon its gory course, its police was already active, but in those days the chaos of orders and counterorders sometimes took our side: my father followed in a dim corridor, saw an open door at the end, walked out into a side street and made his way to the Crimea with a knapsack he had ordered his valet Osip to bring him to a secluded corner and a package of caviar sandwiches which good Nikolay Andreevich, our cook, had added of his own accord. From mid-1918 to the beginning of 1919, in an interval between two occupations by the Bolshevists, and in constant friction with trigger-happy elements in Denikin's army, he was Minister of Justice ("of minimal justice" as he used to say wryly) in one of the Regional Governments, the Crimean one. In 1919, he went into voluntary exile, living first in London, then in Berlin where, in collaboration with Hessen, he edited the liberal émigré daily *Rul'* ("Rudder") until his assassination in 1922 by a sinister ruffian whom, during World War Two, Hitler made administrator of émigré Russian affairs.

He wrote prolifically, mainly on political and criminological subjects. He knew *à fond* the prose and poetry of several countries, knew by heart hundreds of verses (his favourite Russian poets were Pushkin, Tyutchev, and Fet—he published a fine essay on the latter), was an authority on Dickens, and, besides Flaubert, prized highly Stendhal, Balzac, and Zola, three detestable mediocrities from *my* point of view. He used to confess that the creation of a story or poem, *any* story or poem, was to him as incomprehensible a miracle as the construction of an electric machine. On the other hand, he had no trouble at all in writing on juristic and political matters. He had a correct, albeit rather monotonous style, which today, despite all those old-world metaphors of classical education and grandiloquent clichés of Russian journalism has—at least to my jaded ear—an attractive gray dignity of its own, in extraordinary contrast (as if belonging to some older and poorer relative) to his colourful, quaint, often poetical, and sometimes ribald, everyday utterances. The preserved drafts of some of his proclamations (beginning "Grazhdane!", meaning "Citoyens!") and editorials are penned in a copy-book-slanted, beautifully sleek, unbelievably regular hand, almost free of corrections, a purity, a certainty, a mind-and-matter cofunction that I find amusing to compare to my own mousy hand and messy drafts, to the massacrous revisions and rewritings, and new revisions, of the very lines in which I am taking two hours now to describe a two-minute run of his flawless handwriting. His drafts were the fair copies of immediate thought. In this manner, he wrote, with phenomenal ease and rapidity (sitting uncomfortably at a child's desk in the classroom of a mournful palace) the text of the abdication of Grand Duke Mihail (next in line of succession after the Tsar had renounced his and his son's throne). No wonder he was also an admirable speaker, an "English style" cool orator, who eschewed the meat-chopping gesture and rhetorical bark of the demagogue; here, too, the ridiculous cacologist I am, when not having a typed sheet before me, has inherited nothing.

Only recently have I read for the first time his important *Sbornik statey po ugolovnomu pravu* (a collection of articles on criminal law), published in 1904 in St. Petersburg, of which a very rare, possibly unique copy (formerly the property of a "Mihail Evgrafovich Hodunov", as stamped in violet ink on the flyleaf) was given me by a kind traveller, Andrew Field, who bought it in a secondhand bookshop, on his visit to Russia in 1963. It is a volume of 316 pages containing nineteen papers. In one of these ("Carnal Crimes", written in 1902), my father discusses, rather prophetically in a certain odd sense, cases (in London) "of little girls *à l'âge le plus tendre (v nezhneyshem vozraste)*, i.e. from eight to twelve years, being sacrificed to lechers (*slastolyubtsam*)". In the same essay he reveals a very liberal and "modern" approach to various abnormal practices, incidentally coining a convenient Russian word for "homosexual": *ravnopoliy*.

It would be impossible to list the literally thousands of his articles in various periodicals, such as *Rech'* or *Pravo*. Elsewhere I have spoken of his historically interesting book about a wartime semiofficial visit to England. Some of his memoirs pertaining to the 1917-19 period have appeared in the *Arhiv russkoy revolyutsii*, published by Hessen in Berlin. On 16 January 1920, he delivered a lecture at King's College, London, on "Soviet Rule and Russia's Future", which was published a week later in the Supplement to *The New Commonwealth*, No. 15 (neatly pasted in my mother's album). In the spring of the same year I learned by heart most of it when preparing to speak against Bolshevism at a Union debate in Cambridge; the (victorious) apologist was a man from *The Manchester Guardian;* I forget his name, but recall drying up utterly after reciting what I had memorized, and that was my first and last political speech. A couple of months before my father's death, the émigré review *Teatr i zhizn'* ("Theater and Life") started to serialize his boyhood recollections (he and I are overlapping now—too briefly). I find therein excellently described the terrible tantrums of his pedantic master of Latin at the Third Gymnasium, as well as my father's very early, and lifelong, passion for the opera: he must have heard practically every first-rate European singer between 1880 and 1922, and although unable to play anything (except very majestically the first chords of the "Ruslan" overture) remembered every note of his favourite operas. Along this vibrant string a melodious gene that missed me glides through my father from the sixteenth-century organist Wolfgang Graun to my son.

127

NOTES

1. *Rech'* ("Speech") was the daily paper of the Kadet party and was published in St. Petersburg, 1906-17.

2. Ainazi in Latvian, Hainasch in German. Pernov, mentioned in the same sentence, is Estonian Parnu, German Pernau.

3. The name "Kadet" is formed from the initial letters of the words *Konstitutsionnyj Demokrat,* i.e. Constitutional Democrat. The Kadet Party was formed by left-wing liberals in 1905.

4. Kukol'nik is a minor Russian writer of the first half of the nineteenth century who is best remembered for the scorn and condescension with which he treated his contemporaries and "rivals", Pushkin and Gogol.

5. "Black Hundreds" (*Chernosotentsy*) was the name given in the early twentieth century to members of fascist-type, nationalistic groups who claimed to be defending the Russian state, church, and society from "foreign" influences. They made violent attacks on Jews, students, and liberals and are believed to have had the approval of the Court.

6. *Pravo,* a daily paper published in St. Petersburg from 8 November 1898 to 10 October 1917, by a group of lawyers of liberal views; it dealt with theoretical and practical problems of law.
   Novaya Zhizn' ("New Life") was a daily newspaper of the Social Democrat Internationalists published in St. Petersburg (Petrograd) May 1917 - July 1918. Maxim Gor'ky was on its editorial board. Up to October 1917 the paper was critical both of the Provisional Government and the Bolsheviks.

7. Zimmerwald, a village near Berne, Switzerland, was the scene of an international Socialist conference in September 1915, at which it was resolved to seek an immediate peace without annexations.

8. The Vyborg proclamation or manifesto ("To the people from the people's representatives") was drafted by Miliukov and completed by representatives of the Kadets, Trudoviks, and Mensheviks on 10 July 1906, in protest against the dissolution of the Duma.

9. General Krymov was commanding the 3rd Cavalry Corps and was due to march on St. Petersburg. He shot himself when it seemed clear to him that Kornilov's plan was doomed to failure.

10. *Novoe Vremya*, a widely read conservative paper, was a St. Petersburg daily, 1868-1917. It was closed down for attacking the Bolsheviks after October.

11. In 1913 in Kiev M. Bejlis, a Jew, was accused of murdering a Russian boy. The case lasted over two years and aroused political passions and anti-Semitism.

12. Popular name for a much feared St. Petersburg prison built in 1892, whose two main blocks formed a cross. After 1905 the inmates were largely political prisoners.

GLOSSARY
OF PRINCIPAL
NAMES

ALEKSEEV, Mikhail Vasil'evich (1857-1918)

    General of Infantry. He served in the Russo-Turkish war, 1877-78, and in 1899 became professor of Military History at the Military Academy. He then served in the Russo-Japanese war, 1904-5. In 1914 he was Chief of Staff on North West front, becoming Commander-in-Chief on the same front in 1915. In August 1915 he was appointed Chief of Staff to the Supreme Commander (Nicholas II) and was virtually Supreme Commander. He had contacts with liberal politicians, and in 1917 advised Nicholas II to abdicate in favour of his son. He was appointed Supreme Commander by the Provisional Government but was replaced in June and made Military Adviser to the Government. After the Bolshevik revolution he joined the anti-Bolshevik forces, and died in Ekaterinodar.

AVKSTENT'EV, Nikolaj Dmitrievich (1878-1943)

    One of the leaders of the Socialist Revolutionaries. From 1907-17 he was out of Russia. In 1917 he was a member of the Executive Committee of the St. Petersburg Soviet and in July and August Minister of the Interior in the Provisional Government. He also became Chairman of the Temporary Council of the Russian Republic. He opposed the Bolsheviks and after the October revolution went to the Volga region and then to Siberia. In 1918 he was a member of the Ufa Directory. Soon after, he emigrated to Paris.

BONCH-BRUEVICH, Vladimir Dmitrievich (1873-1955)

    Historian, politician, ethnographer, specialist in literature. In 1892 he joined Moscow Marxist circles and helped to organize an underground press. He had a hand in organizing the central library and archives of the Central Committee of the Russian Social Democratic Labour Party in Geneva in 1904. In 1917-1920 he was one of the heads of the secretariat of the People's Commissars. Later he became founder and director of the State Literature Museum (1930). In 1946 he was director of the Academy of Science's Museum of the History of Religion.

BRUSILOV, Aleksej Alekseevich (1853-1926)

Cavalry General. He served in the Caucasus during Russo-Turkish war, 1877-78 and in 1912-13 was Commander of Warsaw Military District. In first years of first World War he commanded 8th Army, in 1916 led Russian forces on South West front and broke through Austro-German line. In 1917 he was appointed Supreme Commander by the Provisional Government but was later replaced by Kornilov and called to St. Petersburg as special adviser to the Government. He joined the Red Army in 1920 and served in the People's Commissariat of Military Affairs, then as Inspector of Cavalry, 1923-24.

CHERNOV, Viktor Mikhailovich (1876-1952)

One of the leaders and theorists of the Socialist Revolutionaries and editor of their newspaper *"Revolutsionnaya Rossiya"*. He attended the Zimmerwald conference in 1915. In 1917, he became Minister of Agriculture in the first and second Provisional Governments, and was elected chairman of the Constituent Assembly in January 1918. He later helped to organize anti-Bolshevik riots in the Volga region, and emigrated in 1920. He died in the U.S.A.

CHKEIDZE, Nikolaj Semyonovich (1864-1926)

Journalist by profession, and one of the leaders of the Mensheviks. He was a member of the 3rd and 4th State Dumas. In February-August 1917 he was chairman of the Petrograd (St. Petersburg) Soviet of Workers' and Soldiers' Deputies and of the first All-Russia Central Executive Committee. After the Bolshevik revolution he became head of the Constituent Assembly of Georgia, but with the entry of the Bolsheviks into Georgia he emigrated to Paris and eventually committed suicide.

132

DAN (GURVICH), Fydor Il'ich (1871-1947)

Publicist and one of the Menshevik leaders. A doctor by profession. He entered the Social-Democrat movement in 1894, was arrested in 1896, and in 1899 was banished for three years. In 1901 he went to Berlin, later returned to Russia, was again arrested and sent to Eastern Siberia. In 1903 he went abroad again. He became a member of the Executive Committee of the Petrograd Soviet and of the Presidium of the first Central Executive Committee. After the Bolshevik revolution he worked for a time as a doctor with People's Commissariat of Health, but in 1922 was exiled as an enemy of the Soviet Government and went to Berlin. He lived in the U.S.A. from 1941-47 and edited the journal, *Novyj Put'* ("New Way").

DOLGORUKOV, Prince Pavel Dmitrievich (1866-1930)

One of the founders of the Kadet Party and first chairman of its Central Committee. He was a member of the 2nd Duma. He emigrated in 1920, but returned in 1927 and was arrested and shot.

GESSEN, Iosif Vladimirovich (1866-1943)

Lawyer and publicist. One of the founders of the Kadet Party and a member of its Central Committee. He was a Kadet representative in the 2nd Duma, and editor of *Pravo* and co-editor with Miliukov of *Rech'*. From 1920 in Berlin he edited the émigré paper *Rul'* and later the *Archiv russkoj revoliutsii*.

GOLITSYN, Prince Nikolaj Dimitrievich (1850-1925)

He started his career in the Ministry of Internal Affairs in 1871, became a Senator in 1903, and a member of the State Council in 1915. In December 1916, at the insistence of the Empress Aleksandra Fyodorovna and her circle, he was appointed chairman of the Council of Ministers, replacing A. F. Trepov. He took no further part in politics after the February revolution.

GOTZ, Abram Rafailovich (1882-1940)

Once prominent in Socialist Revolutionary Party, he was sentenced to eight years hard labour in 1907. After the February revolution he was the leader of Socialist Revolutionary group in the Petrograd Soviet, and chairman of the first All-Russia Central Executive Committee. He entered the Committee for Saving the Country and the Revolution, was arrested in 1922 by the Bolsheviks on a charge of terrorism against leaders of the Soviet Government, and was sentenced to be shot. His sentence was commuted to five years imprisonment. He later worked with Simbirsk provincial planning commission.

GREDESKUL, Nikolaj Andreevich (1864-?)

Lawyer and member of Kadet Central Committee, Professor at Kharkov University and later St. Petersburg Polytechnic. He was a member of the first Duma, but left the Kadet party in 1916. After the Bolshevik revolution he taught in a number of Law Institutes. In his *Rossiya prezhde i teper'* ("Russia Yesterday and Today") he expounded the idea that it was necessary to co-operate with the Soviet Government in order to liberalize it.

GUCHKOV, Aleksandr Ivanovich (1862-1936)

Industrialist. A founder and leader of the Octobrists. In 1905 he appealed to the Tsar to make peace and call the Zemsky Assembly. He was a representative of trade and industry in the State Council and elected to the 3rd State Duma in 1907, becoming chairman in 1910. From 1915 to 1917 he was chairman of the Central War Industries Committee, and became Minister for War and Navy in the Provisional Government after the February revolution, but resigned in May. He emigrated to Berlin in 1918.

IGNAT'EV, Count Pavel Nikolaevich (1870-1926)

Landowner. Educated at Kiev University. He was appointed Minister of Education in 1915, suggested reform of High Schools, and resigned in 1916 when his plan was rejected by the Government. He emigrated after the Bolshevik revolution.

KASSO, Lev Aristidovich (1865-1914)

Landowner. Lawyer by training. He was Minister of Education 1910-1914, forbidding student unions and assemblies and strongly supporting the old regime.

KERENSKY, Aleksandr Fyodorovich (1881-1970)

Lawyer and politician. He graduated in law at the University of St. Petersburg in 1904 and became well known as a defending counsel in political cases. An adherent of the Social Revolutionary party, he was elected in 1912 to the 4th Duma as a Labourist (*Trudovik*), since he regarded the Social Democrats as being too distant from the people. With the February revolution in 1917 he became a deputy chairman (representing the Social Revolutionaries) of the Petrograd Executive Committee, and accepted the portfolio of Minister of Justice in the Provisional Government; in May he was appointed War Minister, re-introducing the death penalty at the front. He was bitterly attacked by Lenin who called him a "half Kadet", a "Bonapartist", a "most dangerous agent of Imperialist bourgeoisie", etc. In July he became head of the Provisional Government and, after the Kornilov affair, Supreme Commander of the Armed Forces. He fled from Petrograd on the eve of the October revolution, went to the front, and worked with armed forces in the capital but was defeated. In 1918 he emigrated to France. He later came to Australia, where he married. After unsuccessful attempts to attain an academic position in Australia he went to the United States in 1940 where he taught for many years at a small girls' college in California. He died in New York, having been supported in his last years by the University of Texas which purchased his papers.

KHVOSTOV, Aleksej Nikolaevich (1872-1918)

He served in the Ministry of Justice, then became successively Governor of Vologda and of Nizhny-Novgorod (1906-12). He was one of the leaders of right wing groups in the Duma. Appointed Minister of the Interior by the Tsar (1915-16), he was imprisoned by the Provisional Government. Not long after the Bolshevik revolution he was shot by the Soviet authorities.

KOKOSHKIN, Fyodor Fyodorovich (1871-1918)

Lawyer and publicist. He belonged to "Soiuz Osvobozhdeniya" ("League of Liberation") 1904-5. One of the founders of the Kadet Party and member of its Central Committee, he became a member of the first Duma, and was State Controller in the Provisional

Government in 1917. After the Bolshevik revolution he was arrested for anti-Soviet activities and imprisoned in the Peter-Paul fortress, being later transferred to the Mariinsky hospital. Together with Shingarev he was killed by "anarchist sailors", according to Soviet sources.

KOKOVSTOV, Vladimir Nikolaevich (1853-1943)

Landowner from Novgorod province. He worked in the Ministry of Justice, 1873-79, in the State Secretariat, 1890-96, was Minister of Finance, 1904-14. He was made a Count in 1914. A Senator from 1900, and a member of the State Council from 1905, he is credited with saying "Thank God we have no parliament!" In 1917 he was a member of the board of the Russian Bank of Foreign Trade, emigrated to France in 1918, and became chairman of the International Bank of Commerce. He published his memoirs in 1933.

KONI, Anatolij Fyodorovich (1844-1927)

Lawyer and judge, son of a well-known writer and theatre critic. He earned a great reputation as an orator through his pleas and summings-up. He was a member by appointment of the State Council from 1907. After the October revolution he became professor of criminal law at the University at St. Petersburg.

KONOVALOV, Aleksandr Ivanovich (1875-1948)

Manufacturer. One of the leaders of the Progressive Party and later (1915) one of the organizers of the Progressive Bloc. He was a member of the fourth Duma, and deputy chairman of the Central War Industries Committee. After the February revolution he became a Kadet, was Minister of Trade and Industry in two Provisional Governments and deputy to Kerensky in the last Provisional Coalition Government. He was arrested by the Bolsheviks in November 1917 in the Winter Palace but was later released. He emigrated and died in New York.

KORNILOV, Lavr Georgievich (1870-1918)

General. Son of a retired Cossack officer. He went through Mikhailovsky Artillery School and General Staff Academy, served in the Russo-Japanese war, and was Military Attaché in China 1907-11. He had the reputation of being a courageous and energetic officer. He was captured in 1915 by Austrians but escaped in July 1916, and held various commands; as commander of Petrograd Military District he arrested Nicholas II and family. Under the Provisional Government he became Supreme Commander of Russian Forces and in August 1917, anticipating a Bolshevik coup, started moving troops towards Petrograd. He appears to have thought that Kerensky was really in favour of such a move but was prepared to act even without Government support. On Kerensky's orders he was arrested, dismissed from the post of Supreme Commander, and imprisoned in Bykhov. He escaped and fled to Novocherkassk and with General M. V. Alekseev organized and commanded the White Guard Volunteer Army. He was killed during an attack on Ekaterinodar.

KUSKOVA, Ekaterina Dmitrievna (1869-1959)

Publicist and social worker. She was the author of the policy statement ("Credo") of the true Economists among the Social Democrats (1897). She was strongly attacked by Lenin for advocation of moderate policies towards the working class. She played a leading role in the Union of Unions, from which the Kadet Party sprang (1905), and took and active part in the left wing of the latter. She later gave most of her time to the co-operative movement. She was exiled from Russia in 1922 together with other intellectuals, and lived in Prague and later in Geneva, remaining active as a journalist.

KUTLER, Nikolaj Nikolaevich (1859-1924)

Government official. From 1899 to 1904 he was director of a department in the Ministry of Finance, 1904-5 deputy Minister of Internal Affairs and Finance, and 1905-6 in charge of agricultural affairs. After 1906 he was prominent in the Kadet party, and a member of the second and third Dumas. In 1917 he headed the Council of Congresses of representatives of Industry and Trade. After the October revolution he worked in the State Bank.

LUNACHARSKY, Anatolij Vasil'evich (1873-1933)

Literary critic and politician. He joined the Bolshevik faction of the Social Democratic Labour party in 1895. He studied natural sciences and philosophy in Zurich, returned to Russia in 1897 but was in Geneva in 1904 organizing propaganda work in Switzerland, France, Belgium, Italy, and Germany. He later broke with Lenin and helped form the Bolshevik sub-faction "Vperyod" ("Forward"); he rejoined the Bolsheviks and after the October revolution (until 1929) was People's Commissar for Education. He was appointed ambassador to Spain but died in Mentone while on his way there.

L'VOV, Prince Georgij Evgen'evich (1861-1925)

He took an active part in the Zemstvo movement, was a member of the deputation of Zemsky and city officials to the Tsar on 6 June 1905. In the same year he joined the Kadet party. He was a member of the first Duma and, during first world war, was chairman of the All-Russia Union of Zemstvos; after the February revolution 1917 he formed a provisional government in which he combined the posts of Prime Minister and Minister of the Interior. L'vov was replaced by Kerensky in July 1917. He was imprisoned by the Bolsheviks later but escaped and went to France.

L'VOV, Nikolaj Nikolaevich (?-1944)

Active in the Zemstvo movement. He was one of the founders of the party of Peaceful Reconstruction (Mirnoobnovlentsy), a member of the 1st, 3rd, and 4th Dumas, and a Kadet.

L'VOV, Vladimir Nikolaevich (1872-?)

A member of the 3rd and 4th Dumas. He was head of the Holy Synod under the Provisional Government, went abroad after the October revolution, but returned to Russia in 1922.

MAKLAKOV, Vasilij Alekseevich (1870-1957)

One of the leaders of the Kadet party, called by Lenin "the most correct of the Kadets". He was the son of a professor, read law at Moscow University and became a celebrated barrister, prominent in many important cases including the Bejlis case. A member of the 2nd, 3rd, and 4th Dumas, he was appointed ambassador to France in 1917 by the Provisional Government. He stayed in France after the October revolution, was chairman of the émigré Kadet group in 1924, and was afterwards regarded as the unofficial head of the Russian émigré colony in Paris. In his writing he criticized the policy and plans of the Kadet party, engaging in polemics with Miliukov. He was arrested by the Germans during the World War Two and imprisoned for five months. He died in Zurich.

MANUILOV, Aleksandr Appollonovich (1861-1929)

Economist, member of Central Committee of Kadet party. In 1869 he translated Marx's *Towards an Evaluation of Political Economy* and opposed what he considered extremes in Stolypin's agrarian laws. He was relieved of his post of rector and professor of Moscow University in 1911. He was appointed Minister of Education in the first two Provisional Governments in 1917, emigrated after the October revolution, but then returned to Russia and co-operated with Bolshevik authorities, becoming a Marxist. He had a hand in the 1918 Spelling Reform.

MILIUKOV, Pavel Nikolaevich (1859-1943)

Eminent historian and leader of the Kadet party. He was born in Moscow and educated at Moscow University, where he became assistant professor of history. In the first world war he joined the "Progressive Bloc", and was appointed Foreign Minister in the Provisional Government. His note of 1 May 1917 stating the Provisional Government's determination to go on with the war until final victory and its adherence to treaties concluded under the Tsar brought strong protests and he resigned. After the October revolution he went to the Crimea, then in 1920 to London. From 1921 he lived in Paris and edited the leading émigré paper *Poslednie Novosti* ("Latest News"). He refused to co-operate with the Germans during the second world war. He died in London. In addition to his political career, Miliukov achieved note as a cultural historian.

NEKRASOV, Nikolaj Vissarionovich (1879-?)

Professor at Tomsk Institute of Technology. He was a member of the 3rd and 4th Dumas, being deputy chairman of the 4th. He was appointed Minister of Finance in the Provisional Government.

PESHENKHONOV, Aleksej Vasil'evich (1867-1933)

Journalist. A Liberal Populist and an editor of *Russkoe Bogatstvo* ("Russian Wealth"), he was also connected with the Social-Revolutionaries and a contributor to their journal *Revoliutsionnaya Rossiya*. In 1905 he was arrested as a member of a protest delegation to Witte and imprisoned in the Peter-Paul fortress, later being banished to Pskov province. He returned to St. Petersburg and was one of the editors of the Socialist-Revolutionary paper *Syn otechestva* ("Son of the Fatherland"). He was a founder and leader of the Popular Socialists, and in May-August 1917 became Minister of Food in the Provisional Government. He continued to oppose Bolshevism after the October revolution.

PETRUNKEVICH, Ivan Il'ich (1844-1928)

Landowner and active as a Zemstvo liberal at the end of the 80's, particularly in the Chernygov and Tver provinces. He was one of the founders and leaders of the Kadet party and an editor of *Rech'*, a member of the 1st Duma, and was imprisoned for signing the Vyborg Manifesto. He emigrated in 1920.

POLIVANOV, A. A., General (1855-1920)

Minister of War in 1915. He co-operated with the Bolsheviks after October revolution and became a Soviet military expert.

PROTOPOPOV, Aleksandr Dimitrievich (1866-1918)

Wealthy landowner, formerly an Octobrist and member of the 3rd and 4th Dumas, he led a Russian delegation to England in 1916 which included V. D. Nabokov. He became a trusted member of the Tsar's and Tsaritsa's entourage, and founded and edited the monarchist journal *Russkaya Volya* (December 1916-October 1917). He was appointed Minister of the Interior in the last Tsarist government and tried to suppress the 1917 February revolution by force. He was arrested and imprisoned in the Peter-Paul fortress by the Provisional Government. After the October revolution he was shot after being sentenced by the All-Russia Commission for Combating Counterrevolution and Sabotage.

RODICHEV, Fyodor Izmajlovich (1856-1933)

An eminent Zemstvo leader, one of the founders of the Kadet party and a member of its Central Committee, he was a Kadet deputy in all four Dumas. He represented the Provisional Government in Finland after the 1917 February revolution, and emigrated after the October revolution.

RODZYANKO, Mikhail Vladimirovich (1866-1924)

Wealthy landowner and Zemstvo activist. He became an Octobrist and was a member of the 3rd and 4th Dumas, being chairman in 1911. After the October revolution he joined Denikin's forces and after their defeat by the Red army in 1919-20 he emigrated to Yugoslavia where he died.

SHCHERBATOV, Prince N. B.

Minister of the Interior June-September 1915.

SHINGAREV, Andrej Ivanovich (1869-1918)

A Zemstvo leader and member of Kadet party which he represented in the 2nd, 3rd and 4th Dumas, he was Minister of Agriculture, (March-May 1917), then Minister of Finance (May-July 1917) in the Provisional Government. He was arrested after the October revolution and killed by "anarchist sailors", according to Soviet sources.

SHTIURMER, Boris Vladimirovich

He started his career in the Ministry of Justice in 1875. and became Governor of Novgorod in 1894. He was chairman of the Council of Ministers February-November 1916, Minister of the Interior March-July 1916, and Foreign Minister, July-November 1916.

SHUL'GIN, Vasilij Vital'evich (1878-?)

Born 1878. Publicist and politician, and member of the 2nd, 3rd, and 4th Dumas, and the "Progressive Bloc",

1915. He was one of a two-man deputation, with Guchkov, to Pskov to get Nicholas II's agreement to abdicate. After the October revolution he joined Denikin's anti-Bolshevik forces, then emigrated. In the 1920's he was the chief dupe in operation "Trust", engineered by Soviet Security forces (G.P.U.) to penetrate and undermine underground anti-Soviet movements. He was taken to Russia and "secretly" visited Leningrad, Moscow, and Kiev where he was introduced to Security agents posing as members of a widespread monarchist underground organization. In 1945 he was arrested by Soviet authorities in Prague and spent some years in forced labour camps. He was released in 1956 and allowed to live in the U.S.S.R.

SKOBELEV, Matvej Ivanovich (1885-1939)

Born in Baku in a peasant family, he became a Menshevik, was a member of the 4th Duma and one of the leaders of the Social-Democrat parliamentary group. After the February revolution in 1917 he became deputy chairman of the Petrograd Soviet and a member of the Executive Committee; later he was appointed Minister of Labour in the Provisional Government. He emigrated after the October revolution and lived in France where he later assisted trade relations between Soviet Russia and France. He joined the Communist Party in 1922, returned to Russia and worked in the All-Union Radio Committee, but was subsequently imprisoned and "liquidated". He was posthumously rehabilitated in the 50's.

STRUVE, Pyotr Berngardovich (1870-1944)

Economist and politician. The chief theorist of the "Legal Marxists" in the 1890's he drafted the manifesto of the Social Democratic Labour party in 1898. Then he went over to the constitutional movement, editing the journal *Osvobozhdenie* ("Liberation") abroad. He returned to Russia in 1905, became a member of the Central Committee of the Kadet party, and was elected to the 2nd Duma in 1907. After the October revolution he joined the anti-Bolshevik forces and was Foreign Minister in General Vrangel's government in the Crimea. Then he emigrated and edited the émigré journal, *Russkaya Mysl'* ("Russian Thought") in Prague and the newspaper *Vozrozhdenie* ("Renaissance") in Paris.

SUCHANOV, pseudonym of GIMMER, Nikolaj Nikolaevich (1882 - ?)

Journalist, economist, and Menshevik. He tried to combine Populism and Marxism and called himself an independent Social Democrat Internationalist. He was one of the editors of *Novaya Zhizn'*. After the February revolution 1917 he was elected a member of the Petrograd Soviet Central Executive Committee. In 1931 he was convicted of being a leader of an underground Menshevik organization.

TAGANTSEV, Nikolaj Stepanovich (1843-1923)

Specialist in Criminal Law. A graduate of St. Petersburg University where he became professor, he later taught at the Law College, and became a senator in 1887, then chairman of the Senate Department of Criminal Law. From 1906 he was a member by appointment of the State Council and for more than twenty years worked on the Commission producing the draft of the Criminal Code. He wrote a number of works on Criminal Law.

TERESHCHENKO, Mikhail Ivanovich (1884-1956)

Member of a wealthy family of sugar manufacturers, he was a member of the Kiev War Industries Committee during first world war, then successively Minister of Finance and Foreign Minister in the Provisional Government. He emigrated after the October revolution.

THOMAS, Albert (1878-1932)

French Socialist and professor of history. A member of the French parliament from 1910 and a leader of Socialist parliamentary group, he became War Minister 1914-17, and went to Russia after the February revolution to bolster Russia's resolve to fight on. From 1910-32 he was director of the International Labour Office in the League of Nations.

TSERETELI, Iraklij Georgievich (1882 - ?)

He was a social Democrat and Menshevik, the son of Georgij Tsereteli, a prominent Georgian writer. He was

143

the leader of Social Democrat group in the 2nd Duma, and a member of the Executive Committee of the Second International. After the dissolution of the 2nd Duma he was tried and sentenced to hard labour in Siberia. He was freed in February 1917, led the Mensheviks in St. Petersburg, and defended the policy of coalition with the Provisional Government and continuation of the war. He was a member of the first All-Russia Central Executive Committee, and became the Minister of Posts and Telegraph in the Provisional Government. After the October revolution he joined the anti-Bolshevik group in the Constituent Assembly, and became leader of Georgian Mensheviks and a member of the Georgian Menshevik government. He emigrated in 1921.

VERKHOVSKY, Aleksandr Ivanovich (1886-1941)

General. He commanded the Moscow Military District in 1917 and co-operated with Social Revolutionaries and Mensheviks. He suppressed mutinies in Nizhnij-Novgorod and Tver' in July 1917, was promoted to Major-General, and appointed War Minister in Provisional Government. He advocated a reduction of the armed forces and the discontinuation of war, and was retired by the Provisional Government. He went to Army H.Q. and unsuccessfully attempted to form an anti-Bolshevik government with Social Revolutionaries and Mensheviks. He was arrested by the Bolsheviks in 1918, then released, and joined the Red Army in 1919, holding a number of posts. From 1921 to 1930 he taught at the War Academy of the Workers' and Peasants' Red Army, and in 1922 was a military expert with the Soviet delegation at the Genoa Conference; in 1930-32 he was Chief of Staff, North Caucasus Military District.

VINAVER, Maksim Moiseevich (1863-1926)

Lawyer. One of the founders of the Kadet party and a member of its Central Committee. He was a member of the first Duma, and emigrated to Paris in 1919 and worked for the journal *Evropejskaya Tribuna* ("European Tribune") and the paper *Poslednie Novosti* ("Latest News").

144

INDEX

146